The True F

the Most A

of Our Time

Here is the fabulous story of the Dead Sea Scrolls,
the ancient religious documents whose discovery in
a cave in Trans-Jordan throws a blinding new light
on scholars' interpretations of the Old and New
Testaments.

In this startling and immensely readable book, Dr.
A. Powell Davies, the minister of All Souls Church
in Washington, D. C., tells how these scrolls were
sold to the chief priest of a monastery in Jerusalem,
who persuaded experienced scholars to translate
them. With a great sense of drama and suspense, Dr.
Davies relates the astounding results of their study,
which confirms the authenticity of the documents
and shows their earth-shaking influences on established religion.

The most important discovery in many centuries,
the Dead Sea Scrolls may completely change the traditional understanding of the Bible—because they
may account for the thirty years missing in the life
of Christ—and offer new light on the period just
preceding His birth.

Directed at all who are concerned with religion and
archaeology, as well as those who relish one of the
most momentous news stories of the 20th century,
this is a concise and valuable volume for both the
scholar and layman.

THE MEANING OF THE

Dead Sea Scrolls

by A. Powell Davies

A MENTOR BOOK

MENTOR
Published by the Penguin Group
Penguin Books USA Inc., 375 Hudson Street,
New York, New York 10014, U.S.A.
Penguin Books Ltd, 27 Wrights Lane,
London W8 5TZ, England
Penguin Books Australia Ltd, Ringwood,
Victoria, Australia
Penguin Books Canada Ltd, 2801 John Street,
Markham, Ontario, Canada L3R 1B4
Penguin Books (N.Z.) Ltd, 182–190 Wairau Road,
Auckland 10, New Zealand

Penguin Books Ltd, Registered Offices:
Harmondsworth, Middlesex, England

First published by Mentor, an imprint of New American Library, a division
of Penguin Books USA Inc.

34   33   32   31   30   29   28   27   26

 REGISTERED TRADEMARK—MARCA REGISTRADA

Library of Congress Catalog Card Number: 56-9787

Printed in the United States of America

CONTENTS

CHAPTER FOUR: The Scrolls and Christian Origins

CHAPTER FIVE: The Scrolls and Jesus

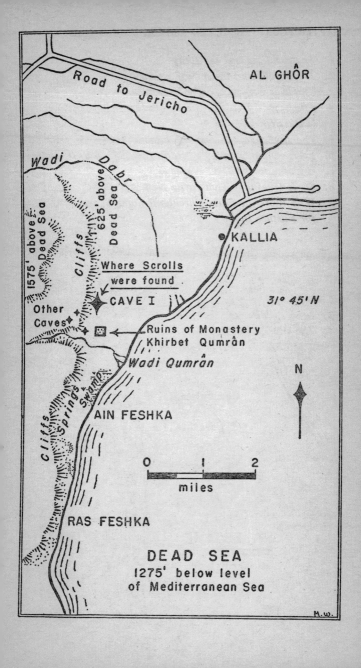

Road to Jericho

AL GHÔR

Wadi Dabr

625' above Dead Sea

1575' above Dead Sea

Cliffs

KALLIA

Where Scrolls were found

CAVE I

31° 45' N

Other Caves

Ruins of Monastery
Khirbet Qumrân

Wadi Qumrân

N

Springs

Swamp

Cliffs

AIN FESHKA

0   1   2
miles

RAS FESHKA

DEAD SEA
1275' below level
of Mediterranean Sea

M.W.

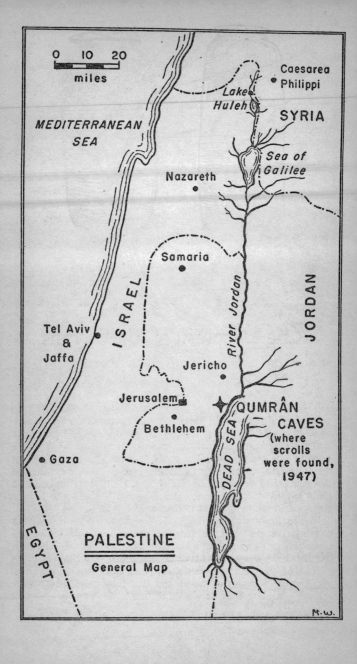

PALESTINE

General Map

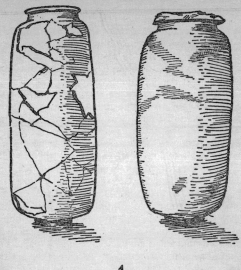

1

The Discovery of the Scrolls

1. The Manuscripts from Wadi Qumrân

Early in the spring of 1947, some Bedouins of the Ta'amire tribe took a roundabout journey from Transjordan into Palestine. It is said that they wished to avoid the legal points of entry at the frontier since the merchandise they were transporting was contraband. The route that they chose took them through desolate country to the springs at 'Ain Feshkha on the northwest shore of the Dead Sea. Here they replenished their supply of fresh water and lingered for a while before going on to the markets at Bethlehem.

While they were waiting, one or more of their number climbed the cliffs not far from the shoreline, and, either accidentally or as a result of a search, discovered a cave. The true details of the story may never be disclosed. It is known, however, that the Ta'amire Bedouins were not without previous experience in exploring caves and that they were astute vendors of whatever they happened to find.[1]

[1] References for superior numbers in text appear on P. 132.

In this region, caves are numerous. At one time, the entire
Jordan Valley was a long, continuous lake and the present
cliffs were then a part of the shoreline. As the level of the
lake descended, some of the channels that the water had eroded
in the soft rock dried out and formed caves. In many cases,
because of the rough terrain, the entrances to the caves were
not easy to see. They were also likely to be small or even entirely covered over so that it was necessary to dig out an entrance. This made the caves desirable hiding places, whether
for men or for treasures that men wanted to conceal.

When David, three thousand years ago, hid himself in one
of the caves of Engedi, about twenty miles farther down this
western shoreline, King Saul took with him "three thousand
chosen men," and went to seek David "upon the rocks of the
wild goats" but, instead of finding him, Saul occupied the
actual cave in which David was concealed without being aware
of his presence there until David himself revealed it.

It was a well-concealed cave that the Bedouins had now discovered, somewhat to the north of 'Ain Feshkha, in the stony
desolation of the cliffs about half a mile above the Wadi
Qumrân.* Its entrance was a hole in a projecting rock which
led into a cave about twenty-five feet in length, less than seven
feet wide, and varying from about eight to nine feet in height.
On the floor, they found a number of tall clay jars, standing
amidst the fragments of other jars that earlier discoverers had
broken. The jars that were still intact were tightly sealed, and
the Bedouins, hoping that they contained something of value,
hastened to open them. What they found they were at first
unable to recognize, except that they were more or less cylin-
drical objects, partly decayed and of a disagreeable odor.

Upon closer inspection, the cylinders turned out to be
tightly rolled manuscripts, ancient in appearance and written
in a language which the Bedouins supposed to be Syriac.
Whether all of the manuscripts were still sealed within jars
when the Bedouins found them cannot now be determined. Of
about forty jars that once stood in the cave, only two have
been recovered intact, but this may be because the Bedouins
smashed some of them in their haste to get at the contents.[2]

In any case, when they continued their journey to Bethlehem, they took the manuscripts with them, intending to sell
them. First, they showed them to a Muslim Sheikh, who supposed, as they did, that the language that he saw was Syriac.
On this assumption, the Sheikh recommended them to a mer-

* *Wadi* is an Arabic name for a watercourse, usually dry but
carrying a veritable torrent after heavy rainfall. Wadi Qumrân is
a deep ravine, wild and desolate, running down from the hills to a
waterfall, and thence a little less than a mile to the Dead Sea.

chant who was a member of the Syrian Orthodox community, who, in turn, sent them on to another Syrian merchant in Jerusalem. To the latter, it seemed probable that the manuscripts would be of interest to the Metropolitan, Athanasius Yeshue Samuel, who presided over a small monastery with an unusual library of ancient Syriac manuscripts, St. Mark's Monastery in Old Jerusalem.

The Metropolitan Samuel was immediately interested. The manuscripts were shown to him, and he saw at once that they were not Syriac but Hebrew. To test their substance, he burnt a small portion and found that it smelt like leather. Arrangements were made for further negotiations, but through an almost grotesque series of mischances and misunderstandings it was July before the Metropolitan could finally complete the purchase of the manuscripts, and by this time some of them had been diverted to another market.[3]

The manuscripts bought by the Metropolitan Samuel comprised five scrolls, two of them portions of a manuscript which had broken apart. One of the scrolls was badly decomposed, and it seemed impossible to open it. The others could be readily examined, and the Metropolitan attempted by every opportunity to have them identified. It was some time, however, before he had any success. A visiting Biblical scholar from the Netherlands, Father J. P. M. van der Ploeg, was the first, apparently, to identify any of the manuscripts. This was the largest of the scrolls, which Father van der Ploeg identified as the Old Testament Book of Isaiah.

Some of those to whom the Metropolitan Samuel showed the scrolls pronounced them worthless. As these were eminent authorities, they have been widely censured. Yet, it might not be easy, even for a person highly qualified to give an opinion, to consider seriously the possibility that manuscripts suddenly produced for examination could be as much as two thousand years old. Furthermore, the Metropolitan was notably reticent when it came to disclosing where the manuscripts had been found. Several of those whom he consulted supposed that they were a part of the library of the monastery and had been there for a considerable time. It also happened that some of the most competent experts, both at the Hebrew University and at the American School of Oriental Research, were absent from Palestine when these initial inquiries were being made.

Near the end of November, the late Professor E. L. Sukenik, of Hebrew University, who had recently returned from the United States, was invited by an antiquities dealer to examine a fragment of a manuscript. As a result, he bought what his diary describes as "four pieces of leather with Hebrew writing" and two clay jars, although he was dubious of their value.

These were among the scrolls that had been diverted to another buyer when the Metropolitan Samuel's negotiations had been interrupted. In December, Sukenik bought another scroll, and at other times, some fragments.

During this period, as so often in the ancient past, Palestine was in a state of turmoil; there was fierce fighting, and it is almost marvelous that the manuscripts came to no harm. In February, 1948, arrangements were finally made for the scrolls to be taken to the American School of Oriental Research, where they were photographed with such film as was available by two young American scholars, Dr. William H. Brownlee and Dr. John C. Trever, who immediately recognized that they were dealing with an unusual discovery and were much excited. Trever sent some of the prints to Professor William F. Albright, of Johns Hopkins University, who confirmed his and Brownlee's judgment that the manuscripts were written in the first century B.C., or earlier, and declared that it was "the greatest manuscript discovery of modern times."

Meanwhile, Professor Sukenik had been translating his scrolls, which he had supposed had been deposited in the cave as manuscripts too worn for further use, just as is done in synagogues, in the room that is called the *genizah*. Here they are left indefinitely, in a sort of ritual entombment, too sacred to be destroyed but unsuitable for further use. Eventually, they may be buried in the ground. Sukenik thought that the Qumrân cave had been used as an outdoor *genizah*. This meant that the date that the jars had been deposited could have been relatively late, though the date of the documents themselves would remain debatable.

By the end of 1948, the discovery of the manuscripts had become widely known to scholars, and in 1949, intense controversy began concerning their date—the so-called "Battle of the Scrolls." Since then, another and even more intense controversy has arisen, this time concerning the significance of the manuscripts, so perhaps the earlier one should now be called "the First Battle of the Scrolls." To both these matters we shall come in due course, as we shall, also, to what the manuscripts contain, but it is desirable first to trace the further explorations which resulted in the finding of so many fragments and the copper scrolls.

2. Exploration and Further Discoveries

In 1949, the war being "over," though not the unrest, various attempts were made to visit the Qumrân cave, which had been rediscovered by military explorers who reported that it had been rifled by treasure hunters, doubtless the Bedouins, who had thrown out quantities of broken pottery and earth in their search for more manuscripts and fragments.

In February and March, a systematic exploration was undertaken by Director G. Lankester Harding of the Department of Antiquities of Transjordan and Père Roland de Vaux, of the École Biblique. They found linen fragments from the wrappings of manuscripts, many small fragments of parchment, and a considerable store of potsherds. From examination of these materials, it became evident that this was the cave from which the scrolls had been removed by the Bedouins. The material, the appearance, the writing, the subject matter of the fragments were the same as those of the scrolls. There was also, in the opinion of the excavators, confirmation of the early date: Father de Vaux thought the manuscripts were written near the beginning of the first century B.C.

Fragments recovered included some from the books of the Old Testament and the Old Testament Apocrypha and some which were not identifiable since they belonged to books unknown.

From the summer of 1949 onwards, fragments of leather were brought by Bedouins to Jerusalem, with writing not only in Hebrew but also in Greek. These were said to come from a cave not in the Qumrân vicinity. The continuous flow of fragments was a clear indication of the need for new explorations, and this led, in 1952, to an expedition to the caves of Wadi Murabba'at, about eleven miles south of the Wadi Qumrân. Here, a considerable store of fragments and many coins were discovered.

Some of the fragments were from Biblical scrolls, others from the second century A.D. There was evidence that these caves had been occupied, not only during the period when the jars had been placed in the cave at Wadi Qumrân, but at several other times, including the period of the Jewish revolt of 132–135 A.D., led by Simon bar Kokhba. These discoveries, in addition to their other significance, are important in dating the Qumrân manuscripts since the writing in the latter is certainly earlier than that of the fragments from the second century A.D.

There was also at this time a systematic search of the Wadi Qumrân region, where in twenty-five of the caves excavated there was evidence of a relationship to some nearby ruins known as the Khirbet Qumrân. Occupants of the caves (or of tents connected with the caves) appeared likely to have been members of a group whose headquarters were the buildings represented by the ruins.

From these caves many fragments were recovered, some of good size. The discovery of greatest interest, however, was that of two copper scrolls, one containing two sections rolled up as one. Although the copper was completely oxidized and the scrolls could not be unrolled, it was possible to see that they had once been riveted together and had formed a continuous scroll which, if laid flat, would have measured about a foot wide by about eight feet long. The text had been indented in the copper and could be seen in reverse on the back, though not well enough to determine the subject matter. Only recently (February, 1956) a process has been worked out which permits deciphering.

Besides the organized expeditions, the Bedouins continued to bring in fragments, and are still doing so at the time of writing. Professor John Allegro, of the University of Manchester, one of the scholars who has worked on the fragments, rather wistfully reports that down to now the Bedouins have received almost £30,000 ($87,000) for such materials and it is likely that they will receive much more.[4] No one can guess how many unexplored caves remain, or when someone will succeed in finding them.

This summary must therefore remain unfinished. We may hear at any time of new discoveries, and although it is perhaps not very probable, some of them could be as dramatic as the first one.[5]

3. Excavation of Khirbet Qumrân

Near the Wadi Qumrân, and somewhat more than half a mile south of the cave where the first manuscripts were found, lie the ruins that have long been known as the Khirbet Qumrân. Connected with them is a cemetery containing about eleven hundred graves. It was supposed that the ruins were those of a Roman fortress, but this did not explain so large a necropolis. It was also known from the explorations of the French Orientalist, Clermont-Ganneau, in 1873, that the graves contained the remains of unidentified corpses buried about four feet deep, with the peculiarity of being partly covered over by a layer of bricks of unbaked clay. Since the orientation of the graves was north and south, they could not be Muslim. But there was no indication that they were Christian, either. They were without recognizable symbols of any kind.

A possible clue to the identity of the ruins had been given by Pliny the Elder. In his *Historica Naturalis,* written about 70 A.D., he mentions that he had seen a monastery not far north of Engedi on the western shore of the Dead Sea. He called it an Essene monastery. Could this be the Khirbet Qumrân?

Professor A. Dupont-Sommer, of the University of Paris, insisted from the beginning that it definitely could: that indeed it almost surely was; but at first, there were few who agreed with him.[6] The manuscripts, he argued, could scarcely have been written in the caves. There must have been somewhere, and probably not far away, where they were both written and used. It is true that Jericho was only seven and a half miles

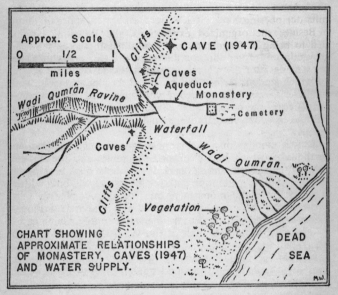

Approx. Scale
0   1/2   1
miles

CAVE (1947)

Cliffs

Caves
Aqueduct
Monastery
Cemetery

Wadi Qumrân Ravine

Waterfall

Caves

Wadi Qumrân

Cliffs

Vegetation

DEAD
SEA

CHART SHOWING
APPROXIMATE RELATIONSHIPS
OF MONASTERY, CAVES (1947)
AND WATER SUPPLY.

to the north, and Jerusalem itself only twice that distance to the west. Still, it was far less likely that the scrolls had been brought from a city to be deposited in a cave in the wilderness than that they were placed there by a community that had lived in the immediate vicinity. Besides, it was now known that one of the manuscripts prescribed rules of order for a community that could very well have been the one that Pliny had described.

Others began to join Dupont-Sommer, and the call to excavate the ruins grew louder. Early in 1949, Lankester Harding and Father de Vaux had dug some trial trenches without particular result. They returned at the end of 1951 to begin a systematic excavation. This required several expeditions but has now resulted in complete corroboration of Dupont-Sommer's surmise. The Khirbet Qumrân was undoubtedly the monastery in which the scrolls were written.

It comprised a main building about 111 feet long by about 90 feet wide, constructed of large stone squares, coated with plaster. The roof had been of palm trunks upon which reeds had been laid and covered with clay. There was what had evidently been a dining room and kitchens, a dormitory, workshops, lavatory, two swimming pools or baptistries, and, most interesting of all, a scriptorium. The writing table, which was of masonry, had apparently fallen through a collapsed floor from an upper room. (It has been set up in approximation of its original form at the Palestine Museum.)

Inkstands, one of bronze and another of clay, were discovered, the former still containing some dried ink which had been made from lampblack and gum. Potsherds were found on which student scribes had practiced their penmanship, and the letter forms were in accord with those used on the manuscripts from the cave. There was also a pottery, undoubtedly the one in which the jars were made which had enclosed the scrolls.

It was evident that the monastery had once suffered an earthquake, which had weakened the tower and broken the sides of the two swimming tanks. It may have been because of this that another swimming tank (or baptistry) was built a little distance from the monastery, one that was visible in part even before the excavation. Exceedingly elaborate arrangements had been made to ensure the water supply, which came by aqueduct from a branch of the Wadi Qumrân. Although the Dead Sea was less than a mile away and its waters are usable for bathing, the monastics, probably for ritual reasons, took great pains to ensure an adequate supply of fresh water.

When some of the tombs in the cemetery were opened, it was found that the same method of burial had been uniformly used, except that sometimes a flat stone was employed instead of unbaked bricks to cover the head of the corpse. It was also observed that some of the skeletons were female, which tended to throw doubt upon the possibility that the community of the monastery was Essene since the Essenes were believed to be celibate. However, we know from the Jewish historian Josephus, that there was an order of Essenes which did practice marriage, and that in this sect, women were also admitted to the daily baptism.[7]

From the presence of a layer of ashes, it can be deduced that the monastery was destroyed by fire, which, as we shall later see, probably occurred during the war which resulted in the destruction of Jerusalem, in 70 A.D. Knowing that the Romans would attack the monastery, the community placed its manuscripts in jars—perhaps this was their usual practice in any case—and took them to the caves for safekeeping.[8]

4. Vicissitudes of the Scrolls

It will be remembered that some of the Qumrân scrolls had been purchased by Professor Sukenik, of the Hebrew University. The other five had been bought by the Metropolitan Samuel of St. Mark's Monastery. Negotiations between the Hebrew University and the Metropolitan Samuel, with the object of acquiring the remaining scrolls for the University, had been initiated but had failed. The troubled conditions in Palestine, now considerably worsened by the war following the partition which established Israel as an independent republic, made all such negotiations very difficult.

It was in these circumstances that the Metropolitan Samuel considered it wise to take his manuscripts to a safer place, and after his monastery had been damaged by shellfire, he decided to come to the United States. This he did in January, 1949.

His scrolls were several times placed on exhibition in America, but no one offered to buy them. Institutions of higher learning seemed unwilling to make money available for this purpose, and such scholars as were interested did not feel that the manuscripts were needed in the libraries of their institutions since those that had been opened had been photographed. The fifth scroll, the one that was still unopened, was so glued together that it appeared doubtful whether it would ever be possible to open it.

The situation was further complicated by uncertainty as to whether a purchaser would be secure in his possession of the manuscripts, since the Department of Antiquities of Jordan had made a claim that the Metropolitan had taken the scrolls out of the country illegally. This was true, if one discounted the war that was raging and the fact that no government was able to exercise authority. On the Metropolitan Samuel's side, it was argued that he had made every effort to interest the Department of Antiquities in the documents that he had bought and that the Department had shown no interest. To this, the reply was that a serious effort would have meant insistence upon communicating with a high officer of the Department, which was never done. The Metropolitan had spoken only to subordinate officials.

This controversy was never settled formally, but the scrolls were sold, for a quarter of a million dollars, to an anonymous buyer who turned out to be General Yigael Yadin, son of the late Professor Sukenik, who had borrowed the money to buy the scrolls for Israel. Some of this money had been advanced by the new Israeli Government, some of it by the American Fund for Israeli Institutions; but an individual benefactor, Mr. D. Samuel Gottesman of New York, repaid both sums and gave the manuscripts to Israel. They were quietly transported to Jerusalem, and in February, 1955, Premier Sharett announced that they would be placed in a museum, which would be built especially for housing ancient documents, and that it was expected that the scroll which was still unopened, the so-called "Lamech" scroll, would be unrolled, and its contents made public as soon as they were known.[9]

On February 7, 1956, it was announced that this unrolling, which so many scholars had doubted would ever be accomplished, had been successfully achieved by a German expert, Professor James Biberkraut, under the supervision of the two Hebrew University professors, Nachman Avigad and General Yigael Yadin.[10]

The two copper scrolls, which are the property of the Jordan Government, were loaned to the University of Manchester by Director Harding of the Jordan Department of Antiquities. Like the "Lamech" scroll, the copper scrolls presented a serious problem. It was not possible to unroll them, but the University announced near the end of February, 1956, that they had been dissected and the inscriptions deciphered. The method adopted was the passing of a spindle through the scrolls, then spraying them with aircraft glue and baking them hard, which allowed them to be sawed by an exceedingly fine circular saw across their rolled-up length (which would be their width, if unrolled), and the resulting strips were available to be photographed.[11]

The multitude of fragments are for the most part in the Palestine Museum, in Jerusalem, where it will be many years before they are sorted out, fitted together (where this is possible) and identified.

5. What the Scrolls Contain

The number of scrolls or portions of scrolls which the Bedouins removed from the Qumrân cave in 1947, may be counted as eleven. Only six of these are separate compositions. There are two versions, however, of one of the compositions, which make, in all, seven manuscripts. That is what is meant when reference is made to the *seven* Dead Sea Scrolls.

When scholars speak, in this context, of a *manuscript,* they do not mean an original composition. It *may* be an original composition, but it is far more likely to be a copy. It may be a copy made from another copy, or from a copy which is the result of a long series of copyings. By *manuscript* is meant only that it is a document written by hand. In the case of the Scrolls,* it is very probable that all are copies, although we cannot absolutely rule out the possibility in the case of the non-Biblical ones that there might happen to be an original composition—a possibility which is much greater in the case of the fragments.

The longest of the manuscripts, which is known as the *St. Mark's Isaiah Scroll* (because it is one of the manuscripts bought by the Metropolitan Samuel and kept for a while at St. Mark's Monastery) is made of strips of leather, stitched at the edges to form a continuous scroll. It is about a foot wide by twenty-four feet long. Although it shows wear, it has been carefully repaired and its condition may be counted good. The text is in Hebrew and its fifty-four columns contain the book of Isaiah in its entirety. There are symbols** in the mar-

gins which have not yet been deciphered; perhaps they were indications in connection with the use of the scroll in public worship.

Although the text differs in detail from the Massoretic text, which is translated in our Bible, in the main it is much the same. This is the oldest of the Scrolls and the oldest complete manuscript known to be extant of any book of the Bible.

One of the scrolls purchased by Professor Sukenik is also a manuscript of Isaiah, but it is not complete and the leather is much deteriorated. This is known as the *Hebrew University Isaiah Scroll* (to distinguish it from that of St. Mark's). It consists of one large section, containing (with parts missing) most of Chapters 38 to 66 (the end), and several smaller sections containing parts of some of the earlier chapters. The

* From this point on, the word Scrolls, when the capital is used, indicates the seven identified Wadi Qumrân manuscripts which this section describes.

** Symbols in the margins of the columns on some of the Scrolls, the meaning and purpose of which are unknown. Possibly, they were indications of a liturgical nature for use in public worship. On the other hand, certain scholars have rather shockingly suggested that they are just "doodlings."

text of this scroll is very close to the Massoretic text used for
our Bible.*

The Isaiah scrolls are not further described here since their
contents are very similar to that of the book of Isaiah in our
Bible.[12]

A third manuscript (from the Metropolitan Samuel's collection) is a *Midrash on the Book of Habakkuk*.** A midrash

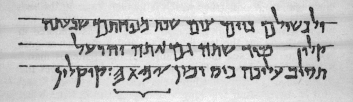

is an explanation or commentary applied to a sacred text,
sometimes in what seems to the modern mind a rather peculiar
way. It is the special nature of the commentary in this scroll,
plus its references to a Teacher of Righteousness, which have
made it the occasion of so much controversy.

The Habakkuk Scroll is only about five feet long and less
than six inches wide. It was originally about seven inches
longer. The beginning is missing, and, here and there, holes
have been eaten into it. But its general condition is good.

It must be admitted that the book of Habakkuk was perplex-

* The Massoretes were the Jewish scholars who, for several
centuries of the Christian era, labored to ensure a reliable text of
the Old Testament books of the Bible. Their scholastic standards
were scrupulous and their concern for detail meticulous. The word
māsōrāh meant originally simply *tradition,* but, as applied to the
Massoretes, denoted the tradition of maintaining the purity of the
sacred text. The Massoretic texts which our standard versions of
the Bible translate are chiefly those of Ben Asher and Ben
Naphtali of the tenth century A.D. There was never, however, any
sure way of knowing how near these texts were, in accuracy, to the
originals. It will thus be seen that the Hebrew University Isaiah
Scroll, dating more than a thousand years before our Massoretic
text, brings (as to Isaiah) valuable reassurance. Unfortunately,
this reassurance is a good deal disturbed by fragments from
Qumrân Cave 4 which show that in the case of certain other books
of the Old Testament the Massoretic text is not as reliable as was
thought.

** Three lines from Column XI of the Habakkuk Scroll, showing the way in which the writing "hangs" from the line rather than
"rests" upon it. The bracketed four letters on the bottom line
show the Tetragrammaton (Divine Name) in archaic script.

ing enough already, even without this midrash. In the form in which it appears in the Bible, it could have been written in about the sixth century B.C., or it could be two centuries later. It could be a warning of the coming invasion by Chaldeans, as instruments of divine retribution, or the retribution could be coming from the Macedonians and Alexander the Great. The earlier date has usually been counted more probable.

In any case, in the Habakkuk Scroll, the text of the book is made to apply to other and later events than those with which the writer was concerned when the book itself was written. For instance, Habakkuk i, 4, reads as follows, as rendered in the Scroll: "Thus the law is slacked, and justice never goes forth, for the wicked man encompasses the righteous man." After the first phrase, "Thus the law is slacked," comes the exegesis, "This means that they rejected the law of God," and after the remainder of the verse, "This means that the wicked man is the Wicked Priest, and the righteous man is the Teacher of Righteousness."

This is the first of the references to a Teacher of Righteousness, of which there are six more in this Scroll. We shall consider the significance of these references in a later chapter.

A fourth manuscript (from the Metropolitan Samuel's collection) has been called _The Manual of Discipline_,[14] although a more descriptive title might have been that proposed by Sukenik—_The Order of the Community_. This is the manuscript which had become separated into two scrolls. With the two sections reunited, it would be about six feet long and somewhat less than ten inches wide. Originally, it must have been about a foot longer, perhaps more. The leather of this scroll is of coarser quality than the others, but it has not been used as much and is in good condition.

Among the fragments acquired by the Palestine Museum are two columns, not quite complete, which it is believed were a former part of this manuscript. They belong at the beginning, but another missing fragment is needed, to precede this one, before we shall have the beginning of the composition itself.

The earlier part of the manuscript describes "a Covenant of steadfast love" in which members of a dedicated community are united with God. Then follows an account of "the two spirits in man," the spirit of light and truth, and its antagonist, the spirit of darkness and error. After this come the rules of the order, describing in detail the entrance requirements and the penalties for infringement of the rules. The conclusion of the manuscript is a long psalm of thanksgiving.

The fifth of the scrolls, in this order of describing them, is called _The War of the Sons of Light with the Sons of Dark-_

ness[15] (Professor Sukenik's collection), and is very well preserved. This scroll is about nine feet in length and six inches wide, and still has its wrapping. It describes a rather stylized conflict between the righteous and the wicked and seems unlikely to be a narrative of an actual war. Probably, it is apocalyptic* and eschatological,** like the book of Revelation in the New Testament.

Sixth come the *Thanksgiving Psalms*[16] (Sukenik collection), which, when purchased, were in four bundles, three of them crushed together. The fourth was very difficult to open and was one of the last unrolled. The average width of the pieces of leather is about thirteen inches. There are parts of twenty psalms, very similar to those of the Old Testament. Considered as literature, the Old Testament psalms are for the most part superior.

The seventh and last scroll (Metropolitan Samuel's collection) was called the "Lamech" scroll before it was opened, because the little that could be seen of the writing indicated that it might be the lost Apocalypse of Lamech. Now that it has been unrolled, it is found that this belief was mistaken. Scholars were perhaps too eager to recover the lost book of Lamech (it is not absolutely certain that it ever existed) and were therefore incautious.

This scroll, which is written in Aramaic, not Hebrew, we can conveniently call the *Aramaic Scroll* until some other name is given to it.[17] It contains chapters from the book of Genesis, expanded and embellished by the introduction of material which appears to be derived from a folklore tradition.

In addition to the seven scrolls of leather are the two of copper (not from the 1947 cave), which have recently been "opened," as described in the preceding section, but, at the time of this writing, their contents have not been made known.

---

* *apocalypse, apocalyptic:* from the Greek, ἀποκαλύπτειν *to uncover,* relates particularly to Jewish and Christian writings from about the second century B.C. to the third century A.D., which "reveal," often enigmatically, the righteous purpose of God, especially in relation to the end of the present world order. The book of Revelation, which concludes the New Testament, is a typical example and is often called *the* Apocalypse.

** *eschatology, eschatological:* from the Greek ἔσχατος *uttermost,* τὰ ἔσχατα *the last things,* having to do with culminating events, particularly death and judgment, the end of the present world order and the establishment of a supernatural regime. In the Old Testament, eschatological elements are found early ("the Day of the Lord") and became a constant preoccupation of many of the Jews by the second and first centuries B.C. Early Christianity was equally concerned with it.

We must also keep in mind the multitude of fragments collected by the several expeditions and brought in by the Bedouins, of which it is certain that we shall hear more, as time goes on.

6. Significance of the Discovery Ignored by New Testament Scholars

Until recently, the Dead Sea Scrolls have been largely ignored by the majority of New Testament scholars. The Catholic magazine *Commonweal* (Dec. 9, 1955) suggests that the reason may be that "many of them did not have an adequate training in Hebrew and the Semitic background necessary to handle these texts." In view of the importance of what is involved, this is surely an insufficient reason. Whatever technical qualifications the New Testament scholars lacked could readily have been supplied by Semitic specialists among their colleagues. There have also been, since 1948, an ever-increasing number of informative articles in the archeological and Biblical journals which New Testament scholars are supposed to read. Many of the questions at issue could even have been evaluated by consulting standard reference sources such as the Biblical encyclopedias. In any case, it was a situation that could not continue.

Largely due to the long article in the *New Yorker* magazine (May 14, 1955) written by Mr. Edmund Wilson, the general public became interested in the Scrolls. The New Testament scholars had to begin to say something. And what some of them said was that they do not think much of Mr. Wilson. He is not a scholar, he is only a reporter. What they neglect to mention is that he is a very good reporter and that he has transmitted quite correctly what the experts who have been working on the Scrolls have come to think about them. Indeed, the conclusion is inescapable that the real difficulty which the New Testament scholars have been experiencing with Mr. Wilson lies precisely in his unexpected competency. Theodore A. Gill, one of the editors of the *Christian Century* (October 26, 1955) whimsically complains of this in a review of Mr. Wilson's book, *The Scrolls from the Dead Sea* (which repeats his *New Yorker* article at slightly greater length). Mr. Wilson's remarkable faculty for walking without stumbling where even scholars are known to zig-zag a bit, Mr. Gill finds rather frightening. Of course it is frightening. Mr. Wilson has no creedal preconceptions to guard, no dogmatic pattern that must somehow or other be found to fit the shape of history.

New Testament scholars have also attacked the great French scholar, Professor A. Dupont-Sommer of the University of Paris. Here they cannot say what they do about Mr. Wilson, since M. Dupont-Sommer is a foremost authority and the extent of his learning has to be acknowledged. But they find his hypotheses too bold—too challenging to cherished preconceptions. Yet, he is merely proceeding upon findings in which other experts who have worked on the Scrolls completely concur. Professor William F. Albright, for instance, of Johns Hopkins University, who has done pre-eminent work in establishing the date of the Scrolls, expressed his view as follows: "The new evidence with regard to the beliefs and practices of Jewish sectarians of the last two centuries B.C. bids fair to revolutionize our approach to the beginnings of Christianity."[18]

It is interesting that this statement by Dr. Albright has apparently not brought him much criticism, but when Professor Dupont-Sommer made a similar statement it was regarded as shocking. He said: "All the problems relative to primitive Christianity henceforth find themselves placed in a new light, which forces us to reconsider them completely."[19] M. Dupont-Sommer says "reconsider completely"; Dr. Albright says "bids fair to revolutionize." In any case, there is concurrence; and among the many distinguished scholars who have been working on the Scrolls these two must be numbered with the most eminent.

New Testament scholars are furthermore saying that it is too early yet to draw any inferences from this newly available material. We must wait until more is known and understood about it—perhaps for fifty years. This is indeed an amiable suggestion. In fifty years our present New Testament scholars will no longer be teaching and can hand on the problems of the Scrolls to their unfortunate successors. The fact is that it is perfectly possible to interpret the main significance of these documents already; and whenever a particular hypothesis, based upon the new knowledge, proves wrong, it can be corrected as soon as there is cause for it. It is true that the reconstruction of our detailed view of Christian origins will take considerable time, and will involve, no doubt, prolonged debate. But that is a better reason for beginning the procedure than for postponing it. As for the contention that further discoveries may be made, or new evaluations arrived at, modifying current ones, this will always be so, and those who care above all for truth will have no fear of new knowledge and will not hesitate to make revisions.

7. Public Interest Aroused

It is notable that while New Testament scholars have been reluctant to acknowledge the importance of the Dead Sea Scrolls, there have been increasing signs of unusual popular interest. In one way, this is rather surprising since the significance of the discovery can only be readily understood by those whose training has equipped them to understand it. But evidently the layman is not to be deterred. He senses that there is something of consequence in this discovery, and, if at all possible, he is determined to know what it is.

It can be said at once that he is right. The discovery is important. It is not, however, as novel in its consequences as many people think. Scholarship, when not constrained by dogma, has long since arrived at findings just as radical as those the Dead Sea Scrolls are indicating; but the Scrolls have tangibility and their implications cannot so easily be overlooked. It has long been known, for instance, that Christianity is largely composed of elements absorbed from pagan religion in the Mediterranean area during the early centuries of its development. Even the Jewish sabbath, which both Jewish and Gentile Christians at first observed on the seventh day, was given up in favor of the Mithraic Sunday, the first day of the week. To these matters we shall return in a later chapter, merely remarking in the meanwhile that there is no reason why they should be matters which are understood only by the relatively few.

2

The Dating of the Scrolls

1. Stormy Debate on a Crucial Question

How old are the Scrolls? If, as some experts have contended, they are medieval, then, obviously, they have no relation to Christian origins. If they are second or third century A.D., the relationship, if any, is unimportant. If, however, they were written in the centuries immediately preceding the Christian era, it is at once evident that questions must be raised as to the effect of this knowledge on prevailing views of early Christianity.

This much was apparent to scholars from the beginning. As soon as it was known that one of the Scrolls described the organization of a community with marked resemblances to the first Christian churches, and that another spoke of a Teacher of Righteousness who may have been the martyred founder of this community, the date of the documents became a vital issue.

Scholars might have wished to be objective—as to a remarkable extent they were indeed objective—but the stakes were high. To Jewish scholars as well as Christian, there were implications in the new discovery which might require revisions of viewpoint more drastic than it was comfortable to contemplate. Nothing was certain as yet, of course, but such indications as had appeared were undeniably disturbing. In such circumstances, controversy was inevitable. In the early stages, very little archeological evidence was available and the controversy was thus chiefly between paleographers, accompanied by an attack upon paleography itself by experts in other fields.

It will be remembered that Trever and Brownlee, when the manuscripts were brought to them for inspection, in 1947, at the American School of Oriental Research at Jerusalem, almost instantly (and at considerable surprise to themselves) found indications of an early date. It will be recalled, also, that photographs of parts of the manuscripts were sent to Professor William F. Albright, of Johns Hopkins University, whose knowledge of ancient Hebrew writings is probably unrivaled. In particular, Trever and Brownlee were profound admirers of the work done by Albright on the Nash papyrus, and it was to the Nash papyrus (of which more will be said later) that their minds had immediately turned when they had first examined the Scrolls. Albright replied that the date was unquestionably early: first century B.C., at least; and this was the date that the scholars who first worked on the manuscripts tentatively accepted as they went forward with their explorations.

The probability of an early date was no sooner announced, however, than a counterclaim was made for a much later one; and at the same time, it was contended that the Scrolls were forgeries. The scholarly journals in which these questions were debated lost their sedateness and became unwontedly animated.[1] Gradually, the claim that the documents were forged was dropped because of the impressive evidence to the contrary; but the case for a late date was stubbornly maintained, particularly by Professor G. R. Driver in England and Professor Solomon Zeitlin in America. Harsh words were penned. "I consider Zeitlin's dexterity in debate," wrote Dr. Albright, "as much more in keeping with courtroom procedure than with the objective search for truth that should characterize scholars."[2] Controversy was certainly warm, but it had the merit of stimulating argument from all sides, pressed with extreme vigor, to the considerable advantage, no doubt, of the eventual result—one cannot say settlement.

A suggestion much urged was that the documents came from the Karaites or a related sect, and should be dated somewhere between the eighth and tenth centuries A.D. The Karaites were a Jewish sect, founded in the middle of the eighth century, and were widely spread throughout Babylonia, Persia, Syria and Egypt as well as Palestine. In the eleventh century, the sect declined in the Middle East but made considerable progress in Europe. Its chief feature was a strictly literal interpretation of the Jewish Bible, not only in belief but in what were supposed to be the Biblical requirements for rules of piety.[3]

It seemed plausible at first that the Scrolls might be related to the Karaites. Nevertheless, the preponderance of opinion moved steadily towards an earlier date, while, in successive stages, new evidence, paleographic, archeological and internal to the documents themselves, was making the Karaite theory less and less tenable. The Semitic scholars, understandably amazed and some of them incredulous at first, were absorbing the fact that a discovery had been made that was wholly unexpected and—until the reality itself was known—entirely unbelievable. Scriptures had been found, written in Judea before the time of Jesus. This was the outcome, now apparently secure, of the first "Battle of the Scrolls."

2. The Evidence of Paleography

Paleography, or the systematic study of ancient writings, is not an exact science. It can never be precise as chemistry is precise; nor can it arrange and classify with the precision, say, of botany or zoology. This has led to rather reckless criticism of it, and during the "Battle of the Scrolls," it was even claimed by specialists in related fields that paleography is not a science at all. Perhaps so: it depends upon the criteria. Nonetheless, the methods of the skilled paleographer can scarcely be counted less than scientific. Where material in question can be seen to take its place within a context in which categories and relationships have already been established, paleography can fix dates, approximate within narrow margins, with a high degree of accuracy. Even where these preconditions do not exist, paleographers can examine or re-examine available data in relation to the problem to be solved, and can often arrive at classifications that point to a solution. That this is so is verified repeatedly by the findings of archeologists.

The first of the facts upon which paleography depends is that the forms of alphabeticals used in writing are almost continuously changing. Sometimes there is a drastic change, as from one alphabet to another, although the older alphabet may be used for some purposes or by some writers for a long time after the new one has been generally adopted. When inscriptions are engraved in stone or stamped in clay (as, for example, Persian, Assyrian and Babylonian cuneiform), the shape will naturally take a form easiest for the instruments employed to produce. This generally means that the shape will be "square" and sharp-cornered; it would be difficult to make the characters in such inscriptions curvilinear. On the other hand, when a reed or quill is used for writing characters in ink on parchment or papyrus,* it is natural to "round" some of the corners, thus producing a more flowing or *cursive* kind of writing.

There are other characteristics besides the shape of the alphabeticals which give indications to paleographers of the date of the writing. There are, for example, ligatures, or strokes which join two or more letters together, which occur in certain periods but not in others, or which are found when the same language is written differently in one place or by one particular group than is the case with other groups and places. There is the fact that the writing may "stand" upon a line, uniform in level at the base, or may "hang" from a line in a way that makes the tops of the letters level but allows considerable variation at the base.

There are, however, some peculiarities of written Hebrew which make the work of the paleographer more difficult—and at the same time, no doubt, more fascinating. Ancient Hebrew has no vowels, except as certain consonants were sometimes used as vowels. These consonants, unfortunately, were not always used with the same value or significance. Whether in their presence or in their absence, the word intended by the written signs was quite often not immediately apparent, unless the reader knew what it was already and was using the text as a sort of aid to memory.

---

* From the Greek, πάπυρος Papyrus is a kind of paper, made from the pith of an aquatic plant, *Cyperus papyrus,* found in many places in the Middle East. Thin strips of the pith are laid together, soaked, pressed and dried, whereupon a sheet of material is produced, of durable substance and suitable for writing upon in ink. Many of our oldest New Testament manuscripts are on papyrus.

Ancient Hebrew has been called exactly that—an *aide-mémoire*. Sacred writings had been repeatedly read aloud; and perhaps in some cases, before being recorded, had been passed on by oral tradition. All that was required, therefore, from the written scroll was that it should sufficiently remind the reader of what was already familiar to him. There would thus be no difficulty so far as the original users of such documents were concerned. Difficulty arises when the contents of the documents are no longer familiar. The problems that then arise can be suggested by supposing that in English we had the consonants 'rd' to represent the word *road* but that they also represented *raid, reed, read, red, rid, rood, rode, rude.* Sometimes, of course, the word intended would be clear because of the context, but what if the context, too, contained words that could not be plainly read?

We need to keep this in mind not only in noticing the problems of the paleographer, which, in this particular respect are chiefly those of comparing grammatical and orthographic practices at one time and place with those at others, but also the problems of the translator, which sometimes lead to variant renderings which are the root of important controversy.

The range of Hebrew writings familiar to the paleographer begins with cuneiform inscriptions in Phoenician, or the Canaanite language from which Hebrew was evolved. It concludes with the square or Aramaic text that began to be used in about the fifth century B.C. and which, in its finally developed form, is still used today. Between these two points, sequences of usage can be discerned, complicated, however, by the continuing use of an earlier form, side by side with the new script, at certain periods or for particular purposes.

We can compare this roughly with the use of Gothic (black letter) German concurrently with the Roman alphabet, or with the use of Old English and similar scripts for some sorts of inscriptions (for example, diplomas), when they have long ceased to be usual modes of writing. In Hebrew, the name of God is often written in the archaic script, and this is sometimes the case in the Scrolls.

This, perhaps, is a sufficient introduction to the paleographer's task in the dating of Hebrew manuscripts, at least for the general reader. More will be understood as we proceed. For those who desire a fuller comprehension, it will be necessary to repair to the technical treatments of the subject, which are very adequate but which only the persistent student will be able to follow if he knows nothing of the rather large documentary context and is unacquainted with the peculiarities of Semitic languages.[4]

In seeking to date the Scrolls, the paleographers were most

of all concerned with comparing the script of these documents
with the various stages in the modification of the Aramaic
script (usually called the square script). This requires famil-
iarity with an immense amount of material, an acquirement
which very few people possess. It was because he was one of
these very few that Professor Albright could feel confident of
an early date as soon as he saw photographs of parts of the
manuscripts, but it was several years before he could persuade
some of the other experts that his dating was correct.[5]

There were, of course, many different approaches in making
the comparisons, both in America and abroad. We shall take
as most instructive the scheme of reference established by Dr.
S. A. Birnbaum (a masterpiece of paleographic scholarship)
and used by Trever and others,[6] a general idea of which may
be gathered by reference to the accompanying chart (Pages 32-
33). At one end of Birnbaum's scale is a medieval bill of sale
followed by tenth and ninth century codices (the procedure
is backwards through A.D. to B.C.); then a fragment from an
eighth century papyrus, a fifth century Hebrew letter, a fourth
century papyrus fragment, and an early third century text discovered by excavators at Dura Europas on the River Euphrates.[7]

Zeitlin, the vigorous controversialist who edits the *Jewish
Quarterly Review* (and who is generous with its pages in allowing his antagonists space to reply), thought the medieval
bill of sale (11th century) showed similarities to the Scrolls.
But actually, it is not even written in the style of handwriting
used for books, but in a more informal, cursive style. This was
soon pointed out.[8] Similar argument ended in the same way
until there seemed to be no doubt that the Scrolls were at least
older than the Dura Europas fragment, namely, earlier than the
third century A.D.

There is not much Hebrew manuscript material for the
third and second centuries A.D. (We are still moving backwards.) But there are mosaics, inscriptions, and the like, and
after the excavation of the Wadi Murabba'at caves in 1952,
there were fragments which were definitely dated in the earlier
part of the second century. The indications on the whole were
that the Scrolls bore an earlier form of writing than any of
these items.

For the two centuries from 100 A.D. to 100 B.C., manuscript
material that can be dated is virtually nonexistent. There are,
however, several sorts of inscriptions. The majority of these
come from small stone containers in which human bones were
placed, and may be dated to a period, relatively brief, extending from the middle of the first century A.D. (or a little later)
back to the middle of the first century B.C. These containers are

known as *ossuaries*, and the inscriptions that are scratched on them (usually with no great amount of care) are known as *graffiti*. The carelessness with which the stone was inscribed (or perhaps "scratched" is the word) ensures a closer approximation to the form generally in use than can be the case with the more painstaking style used in carvings. But here again, there is little indication of significant similarity to the writing found on the Scrolls.

Next comes an inscription, this time carefully carved, which relates to the successive resting places of the bones of a king of Judah, Uzziah, who died in 779 B.C. It is therefore known as the Uzziah inscription, dated by Albright sometime after 70 A.D. Comparison with the Scrolls suggests that we have not yet gone back far enough.

Still within the first century A.D., we come to a *dipinto* or painted inscription, discovered by Sukenik in the early 1930s. Sukenik's own date for it was a little before 70 A.D., when the temple at Jerusalem was destroyed, but Albright dates it rather earlier, near the beginning of the century. Trever thinks that this *dipinto* "presents perhaps the closest approach" to the Scrolls, though it is only to the Habakkuk Scroll, believed to be written later than the others, that he sees this approach.[9] Even so, an approach is all it is. (Compare Column 4 and Column 6 on Pages 32-33 and then compare both with the other columns. Scholars must multiply such comparisons by the hundreds, using as many examples of each alphabetical as possible from each document.)

Although there are other interesting indications, it is with the Nash papyrus* that we begin to note significant similarities to the Scrolls. It will be remembered that it was the Nash papyrus that Trever immediately recalled when he first saw the Qumrân manuscripts. When photographs of the manuscripts were published, it was the Nash papyrus that was soon recalled by other scholars. It is not surprising, therefore, that, after a process of elimination, it should finally be this document that was found to be closest to the Scrolls. There is still argument as to where the Nash papyrus should be placed within the chronological order of the manuscripts, but not much remaining doubt that the Scrolls and the Nash papyrus belong to the same period. Millar Burrows, one of the most cautious

* A small fragment of papyrus containing the Decalogue (Ten Commandments) and the Shema' (Deut. vi, 4–9) in Hebrew, acquired in 1902 by W. L. Nash and presented to the Cambridge University Library. At first, it was dated in the second century A.D., but redated later to about the beginning of the Christian era and finally, by Albright (1937) to the second century B.C. Regarded before the Qumrân discoveries as the oldest Biblical Hebrew text extant.[10]

COMPARISON OF HEBREW ALPHABETICALS IN THE DEAD SEA
SCROLLS & OTHER ANCIENT DOCUMENTS, WORKING BACKWARDS
FROM ELEVENTH CENTURY, A.D. TO THIRD CENTURY, B.C. These
examples are not numerous enough to serve any other purpose
than to give the reader a general idea of how the formation of
alphabeticals change from period to period.

	A	B	D
ALPHABETICAL (ENGLISH EQUIVALENT)			
ALPHABETICAL (MODERN HEBREW SCRIPT)	א	ב	ד
11th cent. A.D. MS. Marriage deed of 1065. In British Museum.	א	ב	ד
4th cent. A.D. Liturgical fragment from Egypt.	א	ב	ד
3rd cent. A.D. Duras Europas Papyrus Fragment.	א	ב	ד
Late 1st cent. A.D. Uzziah Inscription (stone).	א		ד
Early 1st cent. A.D. Dipinto (Sukenik) Albright's dating.	א	ב	ד
Late 1st or early 2nd cent. B.C. The Nash Papyrus.	א	ב	ד
Habakkuk Scroll. (Late date within Scroll period).	א	ב	ד
Manual of Discipline Scroll. (Older than Habakkuk).	א	ב	ד
St. Mark's Isaiah Scroll. (Early date within Scroll period).	א	ב	ד
3rd cent. B.C. Edfu Papyri & Ostraca.	א	ב	ד

Scholars must compare a large number of examples and note variations within each manuscript. It may be observed, however, from the chart below that similarity sharply increases as the period of the Scrolls is reached. See particularly the letter M.

*2nd of two forms (Mem Sofit)

H	W	CH	T	K	L	M	M*	N	R	S
ה	ו	ח	ט	כ	ל	מ	ם	נ	ר	ש
ה	ו	ת	ט	כ	ל	מ	ס	נ	ר	ש
ה	ו	ח		כ	ל	מ	ם	נ	ר	ש
ח	ו	ח		כ	ל	מ	ם	נ	ר	ע
ח	ו	חת	ט	כ	ל	מ	ם			
ח	ו	ח		כ	ל	מ		ו		
ח	חין	ח	ﬄ	נ	ל	מ	ם	ו	ש	
ח	ו	ח	כ	כ	ל	מ	מ	ו	שרו	
חע	ו	H	6	כ	ל	מ	ת	ג	ש	
חא	ויי	ח	ט	נ	ל	מ	מ	ג	ש	
ג	ל	H	6	כ	ל	מ	ת	ג	ש	

of the experts who assumed the task of dating the Scrolls, regards the Nash papyrus as "slightly later than the Isaiah scroll and very close to the Manual of Discipline.* The resemblances are so close," he continues, "and the differences so slight, that it is hardly safe to say more than that all three manuscripts probably belong to the same half or three-quarters of a century."[11] (As an introduction to these resemblances, the reader may consult the comparisons in figure below. These, of course, are only samples. It cannot be too strongly emphasized that scholars must make a very large number of such comparisons, checking them not only against each other but against references established from other documents, before they can be satisfied that the significance is real.)

It is not sufficient, of course, to stop at the point where similarities have been noted and the date of the Scrolls has been suggested. It is necessary to go back beyond this point to make sure that there are not similarities at some earlier date —or, if there are, to assess their importance. This was done by referring to the Edfu papyri and ostraca,** found on the upper Nile and dated in the third century B.C. The lettering on the Edfu material was seen to be of a definitely older form than that of the Nash papyrus and the Scrolls.

As scholars went further back (and we shall not follow them beyond this point) it became increasingly apparent that they were dealing with older forms of writing than appeared on the Qumrân manuscripts. The indications were very strong, therefore, that the first century B.C. or a little earlier was the period to which the Scrolls should be assigned.

Paleographic evidence internal to the Scrolls themselves tends to confirm this date. In the Hebrew alphabet, five letters have two forms in the square script eventually developed. One of the forms is called *medial* and is used at the beginning or middle of a word, and the other is called *final* and is used at the end. The two forms and their uses were not suddenly decided upon but grew slowly and irregularly. In the Isaiah

	Medial M	Final M
* NASH PAPYRUS	בהנלב	בבבמ
ISAIAH SCROLL	בבבב	מב כמ
MANUAL SCROLL	לבלב	בבלב

** Ostraca, from the Greek, ὄστρακαν *an earthen vessel or portion of an earthen vessel, a potsherd.* Such earthen tablets were often used by the ancient Greeks as ballots in voting to send a citizen into temporary exile (hence *ostracize*). Potsherds were also written upon for other purposes (for example, in the Qumrân Monastery for practicing penmanship) and are found throughout a wide area.

Scroll (St. Mark's) and the Manual of Discipline, only two of the letters have both forms, Mēm (M) and Nūn (N), indicating that the dual form in the case of the other three was either still in the future or had not yet been adopted by the writers of the Scrolls. (Two of these three were, however, written a little differently when they came at the end of a word.) In these two scrolls, the *final* forms of M and N are sometimes used in the middle of a word and the *medial* forms at the end. But in the Habakkuk Scrolls and the Hebrew University Isaiah Scroll, which are considered on other evidence to have been written later, the scribes use all five letters in both forms and in their proper positions. Thus, within the Scrolls themselves, we can watch the evolution of the form of writing.

We have already mentioned the paleographer's interest in ligatures (the connecting of letters together by a continuous stroke of the pen). This frequently occurs within the Scrolls (and earlier) but fell into disuse within the first century A.D., a minor yet nonetheless additional indication of an early date.

There are also other, more detailed indications which, in this general treatment, it seems unnecessary to pursue.

This, then, is the paleographic evidence for the date of the Scrolls, insofar as we could present it briefly and without undue recourse to technicalities. But it must not be supposed that, of itself, it is unassailable. It is the combination and concurrence of several kinds of evidence that brings us close to certainty. We shall therefore presently consider some other sorts of evidence, but first we must recall what was attempted by speculation and argument.

3. *Argument Gives Way to Archeology*

Before the Qumrân ruins were excavated and it was established beyond doubt that a link had existed between the monastery and the caves, strenuous attempts were made to relate the newly found documents to certain previously known events and discoveries. One of these was the reference to a cave containing documents in a letter from the Patriarch Timotheus I to the Metropolitan Sergius of Elam.[12] This cave had been discovered at about the turn of the ninth century A.D., in the Dead Sea area and under circumstances very similar to those of the 1947 discovery. This time, too, it was Bedouins who found the cave. It is even reported that the cave was discovered when a Bedouin saw his dog go through a hole in the rock after a strayed sheep. In 1947, it was a goat, not a sheep,* and instead of a pursuing dog, a stone was thrown—if the story is to be believed. At any rate, the Bedouins seem to have been cave-searchers for rather a long time.

In the earlier discovery as in the later, copies of Old Testament books were found and also books not contained in the Old Testament. The Patriarch Timotheus, who was anxious to see whether any of the Old Testament texts were in accord with quotations in the New Testament (thus explaining the disturbing disagreements between New Testament quotations and the standard Old Testament texts available) went to considerable trouble to learn more of the new discovery. But he was not able to get the information he sought.[13]

It could have been the Qumrân cave from which these manuscripts were taken. If so, it is natural to ask why some were removed and others were left. The suggestion has been made that those that were allowed to remain were overlooked because they were hidden around a corner or behind a piece of rock. Another suggestion might be that the discovery was made in the hot season when the Dead Sea area is a veritable oven, so that the Bedouins grew weary of carrying the manuscripts and left some to be retrieved on another occasion, and for some reason they did not go back. Or they may have sold them gradually, in parcels, and the reward may have diminished to the point where it was no longer worth while to return to the cave. In any case, there is no reason for supposing that the finders of the documents were bound to take them all away.

On the other hand, so many caves which had been used for the storing of manuscripts have now been found in the Dead Sea region that the 800 A.D. discovery may not have been of the 1947 cave at all but of one of the others. Nevertheless, the report that such a discovery did occur lends credence to the possibility that such manuscripts were used by the Karaites, and that either they or a predecessor sect could have written the manuscripts well within the Christian era. That is to say, this is possible unless it is heavily outweighed by other evidence.

There are also some tenth century A.D. references by the Karaite, Kirkisani, to a Jewish sect called al-Maghariya, which means the Cave Sect. Kirkisani seems to have received his information from David ibn Merwan, who reported that the Cave Sect was so called because its books had been found in a cave. Since David ibn Merwan was a good deal older than

---

* According to Edmund Wilson and others. F. M. Cross, writing in the *Biblical Archeologist* (Feb., 1954), says it was a sheep. It may reasonably be doubted whether it was either. The Bedouins did not leave it to their animals to discover caves.

Kirkisani, we are led back towards the early ninth century discovery which was of such interest to Timotheus, and again it seems possible that Jewish sectarians with their own version of the Bible (Old Testament), and also with non-Biblical books which may have been related to the Scrolls, were active several centuries after the beginning of the Christian era. As to the age of their books, however, there could be a very wide range; copying and recopying could have gone on for a long time, reaching perhaps into the first century B.C. But, of course, we do not know. It would be just as plausible, or more so, on the basis of this kind of argument, to regard the books used by this sect as having been composed (or, in the case of Biblical books, first transcribed in accordance with sectarian standards) nearer to the time of the sect's emergence.[14]

One of the most impressive arguments, at least when first propounded, was that the Scrolls must be of Karaite origin because of resemblances to the Damascus Document (which many European scholars refer to as the Zadokite Fragment), discovered in a synagogue genizah in Cairo, sometime near the end of the last century, and published in 1910. This document was unquestionably found among Karaite manuscripts, and it is equally beyond dispute that its contents relate it to two of the Scrolls.* Long before the 1947 Qumrân discovery, the date of composition of the Damascus Document was the subject of wide disagreement. Some scholars dated it in the first or second century B.C., some in the first century A.D., and others (including Zeitlin) in the seventh or eighth century A.D.[15] When the Scrolls were discovered, the tendency, of course (where the wish fathered the thought), was to date them in conformity with the date chosen for the Damascus Document. A late date for the latter meant a late date for the former, which in turn favored the Karaite hypothesis. The weight of opinion, however, tended to an early date for the composition of the Damascus Document and a late date for the copy of it found in Cairo.

There were many other suggestions,[16] some of them vigorously debated, but, as the reader may himself by now have decided, this discussion, which, within a few years, had become inflated to gigantic size (only the barest summary is given above), was obviously not pointing towards a solution. Instead, it deteriorated into the first "Battle of the Scrolls." Meanwhile, although paleography, as we have seen, was strengthening its position, it could not, of itself alone, maintain an early date. Was there evidence that was less vulnerable?

* The Damascus Document will be considered later.

4. Archeology, Numismatics and the Radio-Carbon Test

The story of the excavation of the monastery at Qumrân has already been told. What must now concern us is the more detailed relationship between what was found in the ruins and the manuscripts that were deposited in the caves, and the evidence available for assigning dates.

When, through the exploration of the additional caves, it became apparent that a large library had at some time been distributed among them, and when, simultaneously, it began to be clear that this library was connected with the community that had inhabited the monastery, the problem of determining dates took on a new perspective. What was now necessary was that the ruins be systematically searched by skilled excavators who could recognize, assess and interpret such material as their labors might unearth.

In other words, the archeologists had taken over and much less controversial findings could be reasonably expected. Not, of course, that archeology is an exact science, although it comes closer to it than paleography and has built up an impressive record. By definition, archeology* is the systematic study of antiquities, the department of knowledge concerned with the remote past as it is reflected in records, inscriptions, monuments, artifacts and the like. Numismatics,** which often goes hand in hand with archeology, as one of its branches, is the study of coins (and medals). especially with regard to their place and time of use.

The first unearthings of the archeologists were potsherds, broken pieces of earthenware vessels. There was no difficulty in dating these approximately to the first two centuries B.C., although there was dispute as to a more precise date. Pottery changes in shape, substance, decoration, etc., from period to period and differently in one place than in another. It seemed to the excavators that what they had found was Hellenistic or pre-Roman Palestinian pottery, similar to other pottery that had been found with "Hellenistic" coins. There was also a little Roman pottery which was most probably accounted for by supposing that it had been left there by visitors, perhaps soldiers, at a later period.

It could therefore be hazarded, at this stage, that the

* From the Greek, ἀρχαῖος ancient; ἀρχή, beginning.
** From the Latin, numisma, coin; Greek, νόμισμα, current (or customary) coin, from νόμος, custom, law.

manuscripts might have been placed in the jars (since the latter were of the same fabrication as the potsherds) during the Hellenistic period, perhaps at the beginning of the first century B.C. It was not certain, of course, that the manuscripts and the jars had both been produced in the same period. Nor was it known whether the jars had been made for the precise purpose of preserving the manuscripts. Nevertheless, the jars were of a most unusual shape, up to 24 inches tall and nearly ten inches in diameter and exactly suited to receive the manuscripts. Whether, after being placed in the jars, the manuscripts were immediately conveyed to the cave or had been stored in that manner in the monastery, it was not possible to decide.

There had been some protest, especially by Dupont-Sommer, at fixing the Hellenistic date so precisely.[17] "It is very clear," he wrote, "that the Judean potters did not modify their methods of manufacture from one day to the next, because Roman troops were garrisoned in Judea. Such a change in their methods must have required a certain lapse of time." In other words, Hellenistic design could well have persisted into the Roman period. Dupont-Sommer was already strongly convinced that the manuscripts had been hidden in the first century A.D., not earlier, and that the jars, too, were probably of first century manufacture. In this he turned out to be prescient.

More complete excavation of the monastery (in 1951) caused de Vaux and his colleagues, who had first decided upon the second or early first century B.C. date, to change their minds. They had now recovered from the monastery Roman pottery of the type also found in the cave, together with jars of the same manufacture as those used to contain the manuscripts, *in proximity with coins covering the period from 31 B.C. to 67 A.D.* Meanwhile, Albright, having examined one of the jars, concluded that the composition of the clay was unquestionably Roman. It was now becoming plain, from what had been found in the cave and in the monastery, that the jars which had contained the manuscripts were of first century A.D. manufacture and that this was the century during which they had been deposited in the cave.

De Vaux wrote:[18]

In common with all the competent archeologists who saw them, I was mistaken in attributing the jars of the manuscripts to the pre-Roman period. They are a good century later. . . . I was mistaken in attributing the fragments of cooking pots, of a little jug, and of lamps found in the cave, to a later intrusion. They all have their counterparts in the articles found at Khirbet Qumrân, and thus are of the same period as the jars. . . . This is a decisive factor in fixing the date when the manuscripts were deposited. This happened in the first century A.D., and, if the cave was a hiding-place, probably on the eve of the abandonment of Khirbet Qumrân during the Jewish war.

When further excavations revealed the scriptorium, suggesting that it was there that the manuscripts had been written, and the excellent potters' workshop in which the jars were undoubtedly manufactured, and when, also, the physical arrangements of the monastery harmonized so beautifully with the provisions detailed in the Manual of Discipline, it seemed to most observers that the problem was virtually solved.

The discovery of more coins, of both earlier and later date, more numerous in the earlier, very sparse in the later, made it all but certain that the monastery had begun to be occupied in about 100 B.C. or somewhat before, and continued in use until some time between 67–70 A.D., the time of the revolt of the Jews which ended in the Romans destroying the Temple. The few Roman coins of later date than 70 A.D. testify to occupation by a small garrison, and it is known that such a garrison was probable because of the Roman fort that had been built upon the ruins. There are also a very few still later coins, but they are not significant for our purpose, since the evidence is entirely that the monastery was destroyed by fire between 67–70 A.D.

It is not very important whether the jars were made precisely for the purpose of protecting the manuscripts that were to be placed in the caves or whether they had been in use before that time. However, it must be remembered that they were provided with specially formed lids and tightly sealed. As to the objection that it is unlikely that the potters would go to the trouble of making jars of a specialized design under emergency conditions, it may be answered, first, that the jars had to be adequate for the purpose, and second, that skilled potters would find no difficulty in jars of this design. In any case, from all the evidence connecting the monastery with the cave, and the manuscripts with both, it seems certain that the community that used the monastery, foreseeing the imminent likelihood that the monastery would be destroyed and its inhabitants scattered, placed the manuscripts in jars, either previously made or manufactured to meet the emergency, and took them to the familiar caves. There they would be well concealed from inexperienced observers and unlikely to be discovered until once again—it must have been hoped—the community could re-establish its settlement.

The time when the manuscripts were hidden can scarcely be in doubt. Although the caves may have been used on a previous occasion for the same purpose, as some have conjectured, the last time when they were so used was undoubtedly during the Jewish revolt against the Romans in 67–70 A.D., and so far as can be told, after committing their treasured library to the caves, the members of the community saw it no more.

It thus becomes plain that the conclusion reached by the paleographers is abundantly corroborated by the archeologists. In addition, there were two further tests. Specialists in the identification and dating of textiles were asked to examine the decomposed cloth in which the leather Scrolls were bound. It was determined that the cloth was linen, that it was ancient and that it was made in Palestine, but no date was proposed. This added little, if anything, to the other evidence, but neither did it disturb it.

Some of the linen was also sent to the Institute of Nuclear Studies of the University of Chicago, to be submitted to the radio-carbon test (sometimes called the Carbon-14 test), which has only recently been devised. There has been some disposition to overvalue the evidential worth of this procedure, particularly on the part of Americans, who uncritically think of it as especially scientific. The Semitic scholar, H. H. Rowley, of Manchester University, who says concerning himself that of the radio-carbon test "it would be improper for a nonscientist to speak," goes on to quote G. E. Wright, whose investigation revealed that three separate tests on a single piece of wood yielded dates of 746 B.C., 698 B.C. and 289 B.C. with a margin of error of 270 years on both sides of these figures.[19] E. S. Deevey, Jr., writing in *The Scientific American*, in February, 1952, concluded as follows: "In general, the method has fulfilled its original promise. In detail, however, there are puzzles, contradictions and weaknesses. It will be a long time before radio-carbon dating is as straightforward as an electric dishwasher."

The claim for the test is that by measuring the disintegration of a sample of organic substance destroyed under controlled conditions by Carbon-14, the date of the substance can be determined within a margin of error of up to 10%. The result in the case of the piece of linen from the Scrolls was a date fixed at 33 A.D., with a plus or minus margin of 200 years. This means that if the margin is sufficient, the linen was made at some time between 168 B.C. and 233 A.D., which is the period within which the paleographers and the archeologists say the manuscripts were written. It may be best, however, to rely upon this test only to the extent that it excludes a medieval date for the documents.

5. Probability That Is Almost Certainty

By all ordinary standards, the evidence for dating the Dead Sea Scrolls within the first two centuries B.C., and for determining that they are a small portion of the library of an ascetic sect, some of whose members hid them in caves at about 67–70 A.D., is decisive. Even by rather rigorous standards, the evidence, particularly of archeology, leaves little to be desired. Those who still hope that the Scrolls can somehow be dated to a later period may persist in this hope regardless of the evidence. Extreme skeptics may ask for proof that cannot be produced—and that cannot be produced in many similar cases, including the books of the Bible. Indeed, the New Testament in particular is far more vulnerable than the Scrolls to questions of its authenticity. Nowhere is there a relationship of community to scriptures so tangibly attested as in the case of the Qumrân sect and the Scrolls.

The dating of the individual manuscripts and the relation of each to the others and of all of them to previously known scriptures, both Biblical and non-Biblical, is an area, of course, in which much work remains to be done. Dates may move a little, backwards or forwards, but only within rather narrow limits.

What we know now, with a probability which, for all practical purposes, we may as well call certainty, is that a sect existed in the centuries just before the emergence of Christianity which was organized in ways that suggest a relationship to the early Christian churches; that this community had scriptures upon which Christian writers drew in composing their own scriptures; that there were practices, including sacraments, which foreshadow Christian practices; that there was an expectation of a Messiah to whom the sect looked forward, and a Teacher, probably martyred, to whom the sect looked back, just as in both cases the Christians did. There are many further similarities.

The date of the Scrolls having been fixed within limits which suggest their significance for Christian origins, and the relationship of the Scrolls to the Qumrân community having been established in ways that make this community of special interest in forming our views of early Christianity, it is now appropriate that we learn something more about this sect, to equip ourselves for understanding the fuller import of the new discoveries.

3

The Sect of the Scrolls

1. The Elite of a Chosen People

To understand the monastics who wrote and used the Scrolls, it is necessary to see them as they saw themselves. To their contemporaries in the divided Macedonian Empire of Seleucids and Ptolemies, as later in the vast imperium of the Romans, they were an insignificant little Jewish sect, without power or influence and with no possible importance for history. But this was not in the least the view that the sect took of itself. On the contrary, its members saw themselves as destined to play a leading part in events that would change history so profoundly that the existing world order would be brought to an end and a new and very different one inaugurated.

Indeed, it might be said that the sect identified itself not only with a culminating role in history but even with a pivotal position in the entire drama of the cosmos. The Jews were God's chosen people with whom he had made an exclusive covenant. Not all Jews, however, were faithful to this covenant. Many of them, as our sectarians saw it, did not even understand rightly the provisions that the covenant enjoined. It was therefore this particular sect of the chosen people that God would use "to prepare the way in the wilderness" for the new world order which he would bring about through his "Anointed One," the divinely appointed ruler of Israel—and through Israel, of all mankind.

Only this sect, it was held, among the religious parties in Israel, correctly understood "the law and the prophets," and was able to interpret aright the Jewish holy scriptures. The sect had its own library, maintained and increased by copying and recopying; and in addition, there were its own sectarian writings. This library was the sect's peculiar treasure. It interpreted the past; it made plain the meaning of contemporary events; it prophesied the future. It provided with precision for the way of life the members of the sect must follow. All was of God; he had commanded it. This is

43

how the community saw itself, an elite among God's chosen
people.

What we are dealing with, therefore, in the Qumrân community is a highly specialized religious society. Since it is
important to know something of the conditions out of which
it arose and the previous history that had shaped it, the next
few pages go rather a long way back, and then, more particularly, to the last four centuries before the Christian era.

We shall need to note, as we go along, not only the actual
history which led to the Judaism of the Hellenistic and Roman
period, but also this history as the sectarians understood it.
The two are by no means the same. Besides seeing history
from the standpoint of Jewish nationalism and treating myth
as literal truth and legend as fact, the sectarians had their
own particularistic interpretation of their national saga. Their
reliance, of course, was upon their scriptures and the traditions they had received. Of secular history they knew almost
nothing and considered it of no consequence. They were sure
that the truth had been given them by God, and that it was
recorded in their books.

Let us see, then, what it was that had gone before, and
how, after the march of centuries, the Qumrân community
had learned to understand it.

2. The People of the Sinai Covenant

The ancient Hebrews were a nomadic, Semitic people whose
early origins are unknown. Concerning the meaning of the
name itself we have nothing but guesses, the most probable
of which is that it designates a people who have "crossed
over"* from one well-defined region to another, perhaps
from east of the Euphrates to the west, but it is not possible
to be sure.

Until recently, it was the tendency of modern scholarship
to regard the Patriarchs (Abraham, Isaac, Jacob and his
twelve sons, etc.) as purely mythical figures, but it now
seems more likely that they were actual persons of whom
we know little or nothing except as history may suggest itself
through the heavy veil of legend. We may be reasonably
sure, however, that they were not worshipers of the God
Jehovah any more than other Hebrews were until the time
of Moses. The account of them given in the Bible was not
committed to writing until many centuries later, when the
Hebrews had been long established in Palestine and the re-

* From עבר as verb or preposition, *those who have come
across or who belong to the land across.*

ligion of Jehovah had had time to revise traditions which, until then, had been handed down orally.[1] To the Jews of the late Biblical period, such as the Qumrân sectarians, this, of course, was not known. They accepted the patriarchal narrative as history and regarded their ancestral heroes as having been chosen by the one and only God to be the progenitors of a covenanted people. In the same way, they took the stories of creation and of a great flood to be literal fact, though actually they are myths borrowed from the Babylonians.[2]

By the time we first encounter the Hebrews, somewhere in northern Arabia about the middle of the second millennium, B.C., great civilizations had already flourished. Babylonia, in the rich alluvial plain between the Tigris and Euphrates, had developed an advanced culture and a relatively high level of religion. King Hammurabi (or Khammurabi: the Amraphel of Gen. xiv) had given to the world his famous legal code, based on the laws of a still earlier civilization from which Babylonia evolved, that of the Sumerians. Much of the Hebrew law in the Old Testament (cf., for example, Ex. xxi) is derived from the Code of Hammurabi.[3]

By this time, also, Egypt had passed through many dynasties and had long since built the pyramids. What influence Egypt had upon Hebrew religion is much less clear than in the case of Babylon, but it certainly cannot have been absent. Canaan, for a considerable period before the Hebrews began to enter it, had been influenced both by Babylon and Egypt and was famed for its culture and its industry. Its dyes, especially purple, were known throughout a wide area. Contrary to the impression that might be gained from an uncritical reading of the Old Testament, the Canaanites were far more civilized than were the invading Hebrews; it was, in fact, from the Canaanitish (Phoenician) script that written Hebrew was developed, as also was the Aramaic (Aram = Syria) which largely displaced Hebrew in the later Biblical centuries. In all respects except religion, the Hebrews owed a great debt to the Canaanites.*

It seems likely that the Hebrews had begun to infiltrate Palestine** for several centuries before the expedition under

* The internal evidence of the Bible and of paleography, etc., has been amply corroborated by archeology.[4]

** The geographical name which came to be used in the Christian era for the country of the Bible (Holy Land) extending from the Mediterranean to a variable frontier east of the Jordan (according to the Bible period depicted) and, at its greatest length, from Dan in the north to Beersheba in the south. The Canaanites occupied most of this territory west of the Jordan.

Joshua. Hebrew tribes were also apparently living amid the swampy pastures in northeastern Egypt, having been given permission by a Pharaoh descended from Semitic conquerors (the Hyksos) who regarded them as kinsfolk. Under a subsequent dynasty (XVIII), no longer Semitic, Rameses II may have employed these tribes in his extensive building operations, under characteristically harsh conditions. During the reign of his son, Merneptah, the tribes revolted and were led by an Egyptian-educated kinsman, Moses, out into the desert. According to tradition, this flight involved crossing a "lake of reeds" (yam sūph)* near the upper extremity of the Gulf of Suez while a windstorm held back the shallow waters. Then, with a change in the wind, the waters came back, discouraging the Egyptians from continuing their pursuit. Some of the Egyptians may very well have driven their chariots part way across, becoming mired in the mud and helpless to move, and thus, when the wind changed, were submerged beneath the onrush of water. At any rate, this adventure marked a high point in Hebrew tradition, the safe passage of the tribes through the marsh being attributed to the direct intervention of Moses' God, Jehovah.

We now come to the event that was of central importance in Hebrew history, the unification of the tribes under Moses through the divine covenant at Mt. Sinai. Not only the tribes which had escaped from Egypt but other tribes from the desert and steppes of Arabia joined in this covenant. They were all to worship the God whose abode had been Mt. Sinai and who had been worshiped by Moses and his family, a jealous and warlike God who would lead them in the conquest of Canaan. The tradition was that this God, Jehovah** appeared to Moses in a theophany and gave him the

* יַם־סוּף means sea or lake of reeds rather than Red Sea.[5] There are many reports, some based upon military observation, of shallow water being blown back considerable distances by strong winds. The waters of Lake Menzaleh at the entrance to the Suez Canal have been seen to recede seven miles under the impact of a powerful east wind.[6]

**The actual name is YHWH, (יהוה) Yahweh, but this name was too sacred to be spoken aloud and therefore the word Adonai (אֲדֹנָי), meaning Lord, was substituted. Where Adonai was used as a preceding word (the Lord Yahweh), Elohim (אֱלֹהִים,), meaning God (formerly plural, gods) was used. It will be remembered that there were no vowels in ancient Hebrew. When they were later added, those for Adonai or Elohim were supplied in the case of YHWH, to indicate pronunciation of the word to be spoken, not the word written, which no Hebrew was allowed to speak. Jews understood this, but Christians did not. The latter therefore supplied the Adonai vowels to YHWH, making $Y_aH_oW_aH$

Law, the famous Decalogue or Ten Commandments, together with other and more detailed legislation.

Most modern scholars regard the Decalogue, at least in the form in which it appears in Exodus XX, as a much later development.[7] If we date the covenant at Mt. Sinai somewhere near the middle of the thirteenth century B.C., it would be at least four centuries later before the ethical level had been reached that would make the Mosaic law possible. To the monastics at Qumrân, however, as to Jews everywhere at that time, it was the most sacred of truths that God had given the entire law to Moses at Sinai. It was this law, together with the traditional understanding and interpretation of it, that was called the Torah (authoritative teaching).

Aaron, Moses' brother, who was already a priest of the cult of Jehovah, helped in establishing the early ritual. As such, he was the original high priest of the covenanted tribes, who, by this time if not before, were less likely to call themselves Hebrews (unless they were identifying themselves to foreigners) than Israelites, the children of Jacob whose name God had changed to Israel. To the Qumrân sect, Aaron was an important figure: there would be a "Messiah of Aaron" at the end of the world order; and there would also be a "Messiah of Israel."

After a period of perhaps half a century, spent in the Arabian peninsula, the Israelites moved towards Canaan. Moses having died in the meanwhile, the new leader or chief sheikh was Joshua. For strategic reasons, they went first to the east of the Jordan. Some of the tribes remained there, fighting for a foothold, while others crossed the river and began to settle among the Canaanites. There was certainly fighting, but it would be mistaken to suppose that the land was conquered. The more accurate word is infiltrated.

As one commentator has stated it, "Religious writers of Israelite literature loved to paint, in glowing colors, pictures of the ancient fortunes of their race. The bulk of the Book of Joshua may be described as an allegory . . . but with hardly more claim to be historical than Bunyan's *Holy War*. It represents all the people of God as making war upon the enemies of God, and . . . the complete extermination of every Canaanite."[8] What actually happened was that a few cities were subdued, and others, because they were too strong to be attacked, were left alone. Very largely, the Israelites settled in the hills, which were easier to defend, while the Canaanites continued to

---

or Jehovah. The word in this conflate form has long been in general use, and, with this explanation, we shall continue to use it.

occupy the plains, until in the course of time the two peoples were merged, with the Israelites dominant.

There is more than a hint of this in archaic fragments embedded in the Bible books themselves (Judges and I and II Samuel), and we may be sure "that the Israelite occupation of the country was a long, slow process. . . . No sudden change took place in religion or manner of life. Canaanite became Israelite by imperceptible stages."[9] Excavations during the present century completely corroborate this view.

To Jews of the last centuries before the Christian era, including the sect of the Scrolls, the picture, of course, was entirely different. Jehovah had expressly given this "Promised Land" to the Israelites, his covenanted people, who, in accordance with Jehovah's will, had wiped out its previous inhabitants and then occupied it. Palestine was thus Jehovah's special territory, in which the drama of world history was supernaturally centered. What transpired within its borders was significant not only for those who lived there but for all mankind, and indeed for the entire cosmos.

The Israelites who went to live in Canaan were not monotheists but henotheists. That is to say, they were not believers in only one God whom alone they worshiped; they believed in a plurality of gods to one of whom, Jehovah, they were especially related. Jehovah was particularly their God of War. (That is the meaning of "Lord of Hosts.") But they participated eagerly in the worship of other gods, notably those connected with fertility cults, engaging down to about the seventh century (and, to a lesser extent, later) in the sexual orgies of the groves of Ashtoreth (Semitic equivalent of Aphrodite and Venus).

The truth is that the worship of Jehovah took a long while to become firmly established. So did the nation itself. From the time of the occupation until about 1025 B.C., the Israelites were loosely organized under local sheikhs, called "judges." In times of peril, one of these sheikhs would take temporary command and form an army to repel marauders or invaders. Eventually, it was seen that this was an inefficient method and, to ensure a better and more continuous defense, the settlements agreed to unite under a single ruler. A king was chosen and solemnly acclaimed as "Jehovah's Anointed."

Saul was the first of the kings, soon followed by the most famous and successful, the beloved David. It was David who reduced the almost impregnable Zion and made it his capital city: Jerusalem. It was he who extended his empire into Syria in the north and far east across the Jordan. Conditions in the great nations by which Israel was surrounded were for the moment favorable to this expansion and continued so during the subsequent reign of Solomon. This was the only period, down to the time of Judas Maccabeus (second century B.C.) when it might be said that Israel was independent.

It was natural, therefore, that the Jews of the later period, including the sect at Qumrân, should ascribe great importance to David. He was *the* king, "the Lord's Anointed" beyond all others. He was also the psalmist, poet, and romantic hero, the beloved of Jehovah, who forgave his sins (including flagrant adultery and a brutally contrived murder) and showered upon him the fullness of the divine favor.

Solomon, who succeeded David, avoided war by adding to his harem the daughters of rulers whom otherwise he might have had to fight, and became noted for his wisdom. But the luxury of his court was a drain upon the country and, by the time of his death, his subjects had come close to rebellion.

It was Solomon who erected the first temple to Jehovah in the capital city, actually a royal chapel, inferior in size and elegance to his own palace, but an important recognition of the supremacy of Jehovah and the first step in the trend towards centralizing his worship in Jerusalem.

At this point, the earlier phase of Hebrew history may be said to have defined itself. Desert tribes had united and become a covenanted people. They had established Sinai as their focal point of history. They had occupied a cultivated land, worshiped its gods, absorbed its civilization, but had accorded supremacy to the Sinai God, Jehovah.

3. *The Prophets of Righteousness*

Upon the death of Solomon, his kingdom was divided into two parts, Israel in the north, Judah in the south, and there was frequent strife between them. Both kingdoms became pawns in the wars and intrigues of the great powers: Egypt to the south, forever either reviving or declining; Assyria, land of ardent militarists; Babylon, hungry for conquests; Persia, empire-builder and civilizer; and from time to time, smaller powers in combination.

It is not necessary here for the story to be told in detail.[10] We need only to see its significance as the Jews of the Roman period saw it, especially the sect at Qumrân. This sect, besides honoring the Law, was much occupied with the prophecies.

Who were the prophets? We must start with the dramatic Elijah, not himself a prophet in the sense that later history would define the term, but a forerunner of the prophets. Near the end of the first quarter of the ninth century B.C., Ahab, ruler of the northern kingdom, had taken as his queen the willful and aggressive Jezebel, who introduced the worship of

Baal of Tyre. This was not unpopular with the people until a drought reminded them that they had neglected Jehovah. Elijah, a fiery partisan of the Sinai God, called for the expulsion of Baal and the assassination of his priests. He succeeded in both objects, tearing some of the priests to pieces with his own hands. Jezebel, too, came to a quick end. Here, for the first time, apparently, we have the emphatic assertion of the rights of Jehovah as the only God the Israelites are allowed to worship. With it goes the claim of Jehovah, not only for sacrifice but for justice to his people.

In the Bible as it comes to us, we have, of course, the association of ethical monotheism with much earlier periods. But we must remember that it was not until *after* the time of Elijah that the Old Testament scriptures, including the Pentateuch (the first five books) began to be written. Most of them were much later. The attribution of the standards of a later period to the events of an earlier is a common characteristic of ancient religious writings, including the Old Testament.[11]

It is easy to see the appeal of Elijah to the later Jews. According to the tradition, he ascended into the skies in a chariot of fire, a signal mark of Jehovah's favor. With the rise of the Messianic expectation, it came to be believed that Elijah would return to earth and prepare the way for the Anointed One, a prediction which John the Baptist thought he saw fulfilled in Jesus but which Jesus said applied to John the Baptist.

"Prophets" earlier than Elijah were mostly practitioners of a sort of self-induced frenzy or ecstasy, an emotional state in which they imagined themselves "possessed" by the god whose incitement to mania they were inviting. Apparently, between priests, "prophets" of this type and seers ("diviners" of obscure meanings and predictors of the future) there was much confusion of function. With altars in many places, scattered widely through the land and dedicated to many gods, nothing was more likely than such confusion. Nor would it soon diminish when more of the altars were transferred to the worship of Jehovah.

It cannot be said that Elijah was not a "prophet" of this frenzied type or very close to it. But he was also something more. And he paved the way for the true prophets who began with the following century. These were prophets, not in the sense that they necessarily foretold the future—although they did foretell it sometimes—but in the sense that they "told forth"* the will of God, interpreting events in the light of religion. It is with these prophets, many of whose prophecies

---

* Prophet is from the Greek προφήτης *spokesman, interpreter, speaking in the name of a deity.*

(sermons, really) have been preserved in writing, that we enter the golden age of Israel's religion.

Even in the eighth century B.C., we still have the worship of other gods besides Jehovah, in both the northern and southern kingdoms. But the prophets condemn it. They proclaim that Jehovah alone exists, that he is the God of all creation. Israel is his chosen people with a duty to worship him exclusively. But besides worship, Jehovah requires justice and mercy, benevolence and righteousness. Unless his ethical commands are obeyed, his altars may as well remain untended. Disobedience to his will incurs his wrath; unrighteousness invites his retribution.

Now the particular circumstances in which the prophets arose—they are called "prophets of ethical monotheism"— were the vicissitudes of Israel and Judah as small nations constantly menaced by great powers. In this situation, the exclusive worship of Jehovah produced two dilemmas which were the constant preoccupation of the prophets, as they were, later, of such Jewish sects as our Qumrân monastics. The first dilemma was that if Jehovah is the only true God and Israel is his chosen people, why is Israel left to suffer at the hands of her more powerful neighbors? The second dilemma is related to the first: if the only true God of all creation has chosen Israel to enter into a special covenant with him, what is his relation to the remainder of mankind, including the righteous among them, and what should be the attitude of his chosen people?

For the understanding of Judaism at the beginning of the Christian era, and especially of the Dead Sea sectarians, the prophetic literature which revolves around these two dilemmas is of the greatest importance. The answer of the prophets to the first dilemma was that the chosen people suffered at the hands of their powerful neighbors because of their sins and their apostasy. Israel had turned away from serving Jehovah, or was not serving him with righteousness. The priests who by now were powerful in the temples of Jerusalem and Samaria (the latter, the northern capital) were too often concerned with their own wealth and aggrandizement rather than with divine justice. The prophets condemned them, and also the secular rulers with whom they and their fortunes were too much connected. "I hate, I despise your feasts," says Amos, the first of the "written" prophets, speaking in the name of Jehovah, "and I will take no delight in your solemn assemblies. Yes, though ye offer me your burnt offerings and meal offerings, I will not accept them. . . . But let justice roll down like waters, and righteousness as a mighty stream." Then he warns that the retribution of Jehovah will be that the erring people will be carried into captivity "beyond Damascus."

The answer of the prophetic period to the second dilemma is that Jehovah is concerned with other peoples, too, and that Israel's relationship to other nations is one of messenger from God and divine servant. On this basis, the prophets address themselves to other nations as well as Israel, approaching, and sometimes attaining, a universal basis. The requirements of Jehovah are in the end very plain and simple. "What doth the Lord require of thee," asks Micah, "but to do justly, to love mercy and to walk humbly with thy God?" Here is an outreach of religion, ethical and universal, that is truly breath-taking.

The people of the northern kingdom were indeed carried away into captivity "beyond Damascus," after conquest by the Assyrians. After 721 B.C., when Samaria fell, we hear of them no more. Their country was forcibly colonized by people from other areas, marched there by the Assyrian armies. These colonists mingled with the remaining Israelites and the result was the Samaritans, despised even in the time of Jesus. But the writings of the prophets remain.

Judah, in the south, survived the Assyrian onslaught and, taught by events, practiced a more successful diplomacy. The prophets were statesmen, too; in Isaiah's case, adviser to the crown on foreign policy. In this far from easy post, the most necessary requirement was extremely hazardous and difficult: to guess which of the great powers was likely to win a war or a diplomatic struggle and to take sides with it. It was also important to know when it was safe to discontinue paying tribute. In these respects, the political wisdom of the prophets was remarkable: it was when their advice was not taken that events took a bad turn, resulting finally in eventual disaster for both kingdoms.

In 586 B.C. Jerusalem fell to the Babylonians, as Jeremiah had warned that it would if its rulers did not bow to Babylonian power while there was still time, instead of depending upon unreliable allies such as Egypt. But this took great faith: the faith that Jehovah was Lord also of Babylon, and would preserve his people, no matter what their subjugation, if they would trust in him and follow the way of righteousness.

Of the Jews (as we shall now call the people of the former southern kingdom of Judah, soon to be known as Judea) who were carried away into Babylon, some "returned" (these were their descendants, not the original exiles) after Babylon had been overthrown by Persia. It suited the Persian imperial policy to permit a restoration of Jerusalem, and a certain amount of Judean autonomy was allowed under Persian suzerainty. The Exile in Babylon had deepened allegiance to Jehovah and had caused the exiles to feel that they were not only the expatriates of a beloved country but also a religious community or church. When they "returned" and became leaders of a revival of their religion and culture, inevitably they brought with them ideas and attitudes absorbed in Babylon, but they also brought with them a renewed sense of the exclusiveness of their relationship to Jehovah.

At this point, we must connect with our narrative a movement that had begun well before the Exile and which produced the book of Deuteronomy (which means Second Law), a revision of the Mosiac law, written as though coming from Moses himself but at a much higher ethical level. This revision was due to the preaching of the prophets. Thus, the prophetic movement not only produced the written prophecies but also had a profound effect upon the development of the Torah.[12]

In the immediate post-Exilic period, however, both the prophetic and Deuteronomic movements were neglected; concentration was upon rebuilding the Temple and its worship, and restoring—actually it was more an advancing than a mere restoring—the rigors of Jewish exclusivism. Observance of the Sabbath was minutely required; mixed marriages were prohibited. The Samaritans in the north who wished to cooperate in the restoration were contemptuously repulsed. Perhaps this was an inevitable phase under the historical circumstances; but it contained little of the impulse of the great prophetic movement.

However, we shall find a resurgence of this impulse when we reach the period that we have been providing with perspectives: the period that produced, on the one hand, the Pharisees, and, on the other, such movements as the Qumrân sect.

4. *The Period That Produced the Sect*

The centuries immediately before the Exile, as we have seen, form the period in which Hebrew religion rose to its greatest heights. The centuries following the Exile, on the other hand, although still producing prophets, were far more the period of the priests. It was during this time that priestly functions were fully defined and codified, and with the rise of hierarchical authority, considerable power was accumulated by the priests of Jerusalem.

Who were the priests? Unfortunately, the origin of the priesthood in Hebrew society is lost in the mists of antiquity.[13] Possibly, in connection with the worship of Jehovah, Aaron, the brother of Moses, who was already Jehovah's priest, brought with him subordinate priests who knew, as the other Hebrews did not, the ritual appropriate to Jehovah. It may be that these were the priests who came to be called "Levites" and whose descendants formed the caste or class whose special function was officiating at religious ceremonies and for whom specific provision was made to insure their economic support.

The shrines of Canaan would, of course, already have their own priests, but whether these were eventually absorbed into the Jehovistic priesthood cannot be discovered. Occasionally, as we know from such episodes as that connected with Elijah, they were massacred. In any case, by the time of the "return" from the Exile, it had come to be required that priests (kohen) be of the "tribe" of Levi, "descended" from Aaron, and, according to Ezekiel, who was a leading figure during the Exile, "descended" also from Zadok, who was installed by Solomon as the chief priest at his newly built temple in Jerusalem.

The entire question of relationship between Aaronic, Levitical and Zadokite priesthood is obscure and controversial, as it was, undoubtedly, at the time of the Qumrân sect, which had its special views, differing from those of the hierarchy at Jerusalem. In any case, during the period following the Exile, the rise of the priestly class led to a sort of theocracy, in which the function of priest and ruler were often merged, and even where separated, the chief priests remained extremely powerful.

Of the first phase of the post-Exilic period, namely Judean history in the last century of the Persian Empire, not much is known. That the country was frequently overrun during the long conflict between Persia and Egypt cannot, however, be doubted, and it was at this time that Jews in considerable numbers settled in Egypt, probably as refugees. At Yeb (Elephantine), in the south of Egypt, they even built a temple to Jehovah, but this was destroyed by Egyptian priests in 410 B.C.

Persian power, once formidable as far away as Athens, was now declining. It was Europe's turn to take the path to empire. With scarcely an effort, the Macedonians defeated the Persians, and, in 333 B.C., Alexander entered Jerusalem. He granted the Jews autonomy, both in Judea and Babylonia, and established a Jewish colony in the Egyptian city that bore his name, Alexandria. For a period, brief but rare —a single decade—Judea was unmenaced and unoppressed. With the death of Alexander (323 B.C.), the time of troubles returned.

Two of Alexander's generals divided his empire between them, resulting in two rival factions, the Ptolemies, centered in Egypt, and the Seleucids, centered in Syria. Judea lay squarely between them. In 301 B.C., after three earlier unsuccessful attempts, Ptolemy I took possession of Palestine, and until 198 B.C. it remained an Egyptian province. After that time, the Ptolemaic empire swiftly declined, becoming first a Roman protectorate and then (30 B.C.) a Roman province. The Seleucid kingdom had no such prosperous early history as the Ptolemaic, but lost much of its territory and a good deal of its authority. Antiochus III, however, achieved a considerable recovery, and it was he who took possession of Palestine.

Antiochus IV, who called himself Epiphanes (literally, "appearance," but meaning "appearance of God"), tried to suppress the Jewish religion, abetted by the two apostate high priests, Jesus (who changed his name to Jason) and Menelaus. In 170 B.C. Antiochus ordered a great massacre of the Jews and plundered the Temple. Two years later, he turned the Temple over to the worship of Zeus and caused swine's flesh to be offered on the altar. Jerusalem he transformed into a Greek city, garrisoned by Syrians, and decreed that Sabbath observance would be punished with death.

This was the signal for revolt. Three sons of Mattathias, a priest who assassinated the king's agent, successively took the lead in the struggle against the Seleucids. Known to history as the Maccabees ("hammers"), the three brothers, Judas, Jonathan and Simon, achieved—though at great cost—a remarkable degree of success. The focal point of the struggle came in the year 153 B.C., when, Syria being divided by a conflict between two contenders for the throne, Jonathan, the second of the three brothers (Judas had been killed in 161 B.C.), was able to have himself appointed the Jewish high priest. Thereafter the Maccabees ruled in Jerusalem for the greater part of a century and retained the high priesthood for considerably longer.

Jonathan was succeeded in the high priesthood and civil rule by the last of the three brothers, Simon, who, like Jonathan, perished by treachery. John Hyrcanus, Simon's son, ruled from 135 to 106 B.C., and it was during his reign that the transition began which drained the Maccabean movement of its religious zeal and turned it over to the worldly Sadducees.

Aristobulus I, who followed John Hyrcanus, made himself king, but reigned for only a year. He was succeeded by Alexander Janneus (let the Greek names be noted: Janneus for Jonathan), who is said to have crucified eight hundred of his antagonists, presumably Pharisees. It has thus been thought that he may have been the "Wicked Priest" of the

Habakkuk Scroll who persecuted the Teacher of Righteousness. After the death of Alexander, his widow reversed his policy and gave authority to the Pharisees. Upon her death, in 69 B.C., her younger son, Aristobulus (II), who was a Sadducee, deposed his older brother, Hyrcanus, and when the latter's friends resisted the usurpation, appealed to the Roman legate. The Romans, now for some time the dominant power in the world, briefly supported Aristobulus, but, finding him treacherous, supplanted him in the high priesthood with Hyrcanus, the rightful incumbent, whom, however, they did not permit to reign as king.

In 63 B.C. Pompey entered Jerusalem.

We should note at this point that it was in the period following the Maccabean wars that the Qumrân community was founded, probably in protest against the debasement of Jewish religion by the Temple hierarchy, and also because of the belief that Jehovah would not save his people until they obeyed his will and devoted themselves with zeal to following the Torah strictly in their way of life and fulfilling the prophetic call for righteousness. It also came to seem to them, as it did to other Jews, that it would be "not by might nor by power" that Israel would be freed from the oppressor but only by a supernatural intervention, when an "Anointed One" of Jehovah would establish a new world order.

Looking back over the past and reading intently Israel's sacred scriptures, new light was seen at Qumrân on the meaning and purpose of Hebrew history. By this same light, contemporary events took on a new shape and color. These insights had been given by God. They must be written down on parchment to be read and reread. And so the sectarians began to write, not only copies of the received scriptures, the sacred books that all Jews revered, but their own sectarian scriptures.

5. Scriptures Not in the Bible

Most of the books in what we call the Old Testament were written during a period from about the eighth to the third centuries B.C., but included fragments that come from documents or inscriptions that are older. A few books are later than the third century, as, for example, Ecclesiastes.

All of the original manuscripts are lost—although it is now possible that there are fragments of original manuscripts among those recovered from the Dead Sea caves. Even in the first century B.C., so far as we know, only copies were available. Some of these must have been copies many copyings removed from the originals.

We do not know how the earlier Hebrew scriptures were preserved when the kingdoms of Israel and Judah were overthrown and the temples destroyed. Did the archives survive? Did some of the priests escape and take the scriptures with them? Did the scriptures go with the people into exile? Who preserved the writings of the prophets? Who did the first compiling, the selecting, the editing? We do not know the answers to these questions.

What we do know is that with the passage of time there came to be many variations in the manuscript copies and a standard text seemed necessary. This standard text was eventually completed in the seventh and eighth centuries A.D. by the Massoretes.* Because many Jews in the period from the third century B.C. onward had gone to live abroad and no longer knew Hebrew, a Greek translation of the scriptures had been made in the third (or second) century B.C., which is known as the Septuagint.[14] Of this also there are only copies of copies available.

The books of the New Testament were written during a much shorter period: from the last half of the first century to the end of the second century A.D., with allowance for insertions and alterations down to about the fourth century. Here again, we have none of the original manuscripts, only copies, the earliest of which cannot be older than the fourth century A.D.[15]

In the period following that in which the Old Testament was written, and in part overlapping it, other religious writings were composed. Often, the form was cryptic, i.e., elaborate allegoric symbols were used which only the initiated would understand. This was partly a security measure in case the writings fell into the hands of enemies. Examples of this style of writing are the Old Testament book of Daniel and the New Testament book of Revelation.

Some of these writings were predictions, especially of the downfall of rulers who were oppressing the Jewish nation, and a prediction which increasingly appeared was that of the coming of an "Anointed One" (Messiah), to which reference has already been made. The prediction took many forms and a considerable number of Jews believed in it, although we should note that there were some who did not.

In addition to these apocalyptic and eschatological writings,** there were also others of different style and content. Taken together, they constitute a considerable literature.

Now, the Bible is an ecclesiastical selection from this far larger literature and is not the same in all communions: the

* See footnote, p. 20.
** See footnote, page 22.

selection made by the Catholics, for instance, is somewhat larger than that made by the Protestants. And, of course, the Jewish Bible does not contain the New Testament. The selection was made at first, no doubt, by custom, and would not have been the same from place to place. But conventions were held, such as the rabbinic Synod of Jamnia, circa 100 A.D., and the several Christian church councils, where the books to be included were decided upon. These are the books which the various communions, each for itself, call canonical.*

Of the scriptures excluded, there are two classes, the apocryphas** of the Old and New Testaments and the pseudepigrapha.† Apocrypha is often taken to mean "hidden" in the sense of being suppressed, and this certainly is one of its meanings, since ecclesiastical authorities had decided to put these books out of sight. But the word can also mean that the writers of the books *intended* their meaning to be cryptic or apparent only to the initiated. There was much writing of this sort in the period just before and after the beginning of the Christian era. Philo, for instance, wrote a book about Genesis of this esoteric character.

The pseudepigrapha, or the "falsely inscribed" scriptures, are not fraudulent; the false inscription is merely a device (due at one time to the prohibition of the writing of new religious works of the same type as those included in the canon) by which a late writer could express his ideas under the shelter of an earlier and accepted writer's name. It then became a sort of literary custom. There did come to be the imputation, however, that these works pretended to be Biblical in character and in fact were not. Thus, the general idea of falsity was attached to them.

The Old Testament Apocrypha include the two books of Esdras; the books of Tobit and Judith; additional chapters of the book of Esther; The Wisdom of Solomon; The Wisdom of Jesus, the Son of Sirach, or Ecclesiasticus; the book of Baruch; the Song of the Three Holy Children; the History of Suzanna; the History of the Destruction of Bel and the Dragon (additions to the book of Daniel); the Prayer of Manasses; and the two books of Maccabees. Some of these books at one time were admitted to the canon. The books of Wisdom and Ecclesiasticus are frequently considered to be of at least equal merit, from the standpoint of edification, as the books of Proverbs or Ecclesiastes. The books of the Maccabees are written from

---

*Canon: From Latin, canon = *rule;* Greek, κανών, *a straight rod, a rule or standard.*

** Apocrypha; from Greek, ἀπόκρυφος, *hidden.* ἀπό, *from* κρύπτειν, *to hide;* thus, *to hide away from.*

† Pseudepigrapha: from Greek ψευδεπίγραφος, *falsely inscribed.*

the Sadducee viewpoint, and history suffers sadly from an excess of hero worship and overappreciation. But then, similar things may be said of the books of Kings or Chronicles.

The New Testament Apocrypha consist of sixteen gospels, five of them of the same general type as the synoptic gospels (Matthew, Mark and Luke) contained in our Bible, but most of the remainder are of a more strongly doctrinal type. There are also some Gospel Harmonies, in which several gospels are combined into one. The five synoptic-type gospels are: the Gospel according to the Hebrews, the Gospel according to the Egyptians, the Gospel of Peter, the Fayûm Gospel Fragment and the Oxyrhyncus Gospel Fragment.

In the pseudepigrapha, which, of course, is much larger than the other categories,* we have some of the books treasured by the Dead Sea sect, such as the book of Jubilees and the very important Testament of the Twelve Patriarchs. It is not supposed that the general reader will want to acquaint himself with this rather extensive literature, either apocryphal or pseudepigraphic, but an account of it is given here so that he may have an intelligent grasp of the proportions and overall significance of these scriptures.[16]

As evidence, the books that are included, whether in the Bible itself or in the apocrypha, are frequently no more important than those that are left out. The reason for exclusion was not necessarily that the documents were inferior in "authenticity," i.e., that they were less true, historically, or less reliable in their testimony. Reliability may be called into question just as easily in the case of the canonical books as these others. The reason for exclusion was the opinion that the books were not sufficiently edifying, or that they were more likely to awaken doubt than to sustain faith since they gave too little support to the officially formulated Christian doctrines.

To scholars, however, these non-Biblical documents have always been extremely valuable. Without them, the reconstruction of early Christian history would be much more difficult. And it is to this important collection of non-Biblical resources that the Dead Sea Scrolls now become a momentous addition. The addition of the Scrolls is momentous not merely because they supplement our previous knowledge, but even more because they require that we revise it. The non-Biblical documents that we already possessed were frequently extremely puzzling; the Scrolls make them less so. There were questions as to whether some of these documents were Christian or Jewish, or—if there were several versions and presumptive

* We must beware, however, of supposing that any firm line can be drawn between these apocryphal, apocalyptic and pseudepigraphic classifications; see Chapter 4, Section 2.

signs of Christian editing—how much of what they contained belonged with Christianity and how much with Judaism. The Scrolls help to settle these questions. They are a key with which some of the closed doors that barred our way to knowledge in the past can now be opened.

6. The Jewish Religious Parties

To understand the nature of the Jewish parties as they existed immediately before and after the beginning of the Christian era, it is necessary to appreciate the considerable extent to which many of the Jews had become Hellenized. Alexander the Great was not only a conqueror: he carried Greek civilization to the entire Mediterranean area and beyond it. Those who succeeded him, whatever else might be said of them, were enthused with the purpose of making Greek culture pervasive of the entire life of the area into which the Macedonians had marched their armies. This meant that Greek philosophy, Greek esthetics, Greek physical culture, Greek ethics and religion had an ever-deepening influence for nearly three centuries before the Romans established their imperium; and after the Roman conquest this influence continued unabated. The entire Mediterranean area spoke Greek, thought Greek, was molded by Greek ideas into what was in many ways—though not in all—a single cultural community.

This had its impact, not only upon the Jews of the dispersion, but on Judea. As we have seen, attempts were made to Hellenize Judeans by force. This was a mistake and had an opposite effect—incitement to revolt. Hellenization, however, had gone a long way in Judea. Jerusalem was to a considerable extent a Greek city.[17] Enough so that resentment was aroused in the minority who still held tenaciously to Jewish culture and customs. It was the brutal and unnecessary campaign of Antiochus Epiphanes, bringing on the Maccabean rebellion, that interrupted Jewish Hellenization, which thereafter remained a national and religious issue, and often a bitter one.

The pro-Hellenic Jewish party was that of the Sadducees, led by the priests of Jerusalem. The name *Sadducee* is probably derived from Zadok, the high priest appointed by Solomon (and honored earlier by David), and implies the claim of descent, originally physical, later spiritual, from the first to hold the sacred office: and with descent, of course, came legitimacy. It was probably not a large party, and contained, in addition to the Jerusalem hierarchy and those immediately connected with it, only the aristocrats and perhaps a majority of the farmers.

The Sadducees took their religion lightly and their politics seriously. As diplomatists, a fair-minded modern critic would not always condemn them. They were practical, desirous of avoiding trouble and extremely eager to be prosperous.

We first hear of the Sadducees during the reign of John Hyrcanus (135-105 B.C.), although undoubtedly the Temple priests were pro-Hellenic during and even before the Maccabean revolt. Under the Hasmonean princes of the later period, taught by the mistakes of Antiochus Epiphanes, they administered their pro-Hellenic policy more adroitly—occasionally, although never for long, being dismissed from power to make room for the Pharisees.

The Pharisees* were the popular party, more concerned with religion than with politics. The one political issue about which they cared deeply was religious freedom; and they looked for national liberation, not through revolt but through the coming of a "Son of David," a Messiah who would not be divine but who would receive from God authority to rule the nations.

The word *Pharisee* probably means "separated" or "scrupulous," but we cannot be certain. There is no doubt, however, that the purpose of separation from "heathen" associations and non-Jewish practices was at the root of Pharisaic piety. It was apparently the Sadducean pro-Hellenizing policy under the Hasmonean princes that caused the Pharisees to withdraw and form their own party, although it was also in part the Sadducean attempt to maneuver for more political independence instead of fostering religious liberties.

The chief differences between the Sadducees and the Pharisees were as follows: 1) the Sadducees charged that the Pharisees taught the people observances that were not written in the law of Moses—which was true in the sense that Mosaic law was interpreted by the Pharisees to meet contemporary conditions; 2) the Pharisees believed in immortality, heaven and hell, a general resurrection, a Messianic kingdom, concerning all of which the Sadducees claimed that nothing should be taught since nothing is known; 3) the Sadducees held the Hellenic doctrine of free will, whereas the Pharisees contended that free will was limited by the predestinate purposes of God; 4) the Pharisees held that the practices of the Sadducees were inconsistent with the obligations of high

* In the New Testament we read of "the Scribes and the Pharisees" more often than of the Pharisees alone. The Scribes were the professional copyists of the scriptures, who were skilled, also, in expounding "the Law and the Prophets." However, they were of the same party as the Pharisees. (They might be called "the Scribes *of* the Pharisees.")

priesthood—which was conspicuously and painfully true; 5) the Pharisees were proselytizers, believing in an international Jewish community or church, into which all might enter who would accept the Jewish law and the Pharisaic ritual requirements, and were interested chiefly in the Judaism of the synagogue. The Sadducees cared nothing for winning converts, and their interest was the Temple and power centralized at Jerusalem.*

It is true that the Pharisees were often haughty and uncharitable. But it is also true that they took a deeply ethical view of religion. Some of the great rabbis, such as Hillel, were Pharisees, and reached, as Christian and Jewish scholars agree, a level close to that of Jesus in their moral teachings.

With the destruction of the temple in 70 A.D., the role of the Sadducees was ended and they disappeared; but the Pharisees, who no longer needed the Temple but had concentrated on the synagogue, survived and flourished, and provided the basis for the rabbinical tradition that endures in modern Judaism.

Another sect, the Zealots, had broken away from the Pharisees, believing that the latter were not sufficiently devoted to the cause of national independence. Josephus says of them that "Judas, the Galilean" was their founder and adds that they "agree in all things with the Pharisaic notions; but they have an inviolable attachment to liberty, and say that God is to be their only Ruler and Lord."[18]

It will be remembered that Simon, a member of the Zealot party, was one of the twelve disciples chosen by Jesus. The choice was made, however, at a time when the political scene was relatively quiet, and no uprising, so far as is known, was then anticipated.

The Zealots were really a revival of the Maccabean movement, and may have been as rigorous in religious practice as they were fervent in hoping for the overthrow of the Roman domination. In the end, they did Judea a great disservice, recklessly inciting violence and overthrowing all moderating influences, until there was nothing the Jewish leaders could do to placate the Romans or prevent the war that ended in the destruction of Jerusalem.

There was still a further Jewish religious party, but since it is the object of our particular interest, we shall describe it more fully than the others, beginning with the following section.

* The Pharisees reversed themselves and withdrew from their missionary program during the early successes of the Christian churches; they also condemned the Septuagint (the Greek version of the Old Testament) because it facilitated the combination of Judaic and Pagan doctrine which entered into the developing Christian system.

7. Who Were the Essenes?

Our original sources for information about the Essenes are Philo of Alexandria (*Quod Omnis Probus Liber,* circa 20 A.D.), Pliny the Elder (*Historica Naturalis,* circa 70 A.D.), and the Jewish historian, Josephus (*Antiquities of the Jews, Wars of the Jews,* written 69-94 A.D.).* Whether they were a single sect, with doctrines and practices that changed in certain respects over a period of time, or were a group of sects, differing considerably in some of their beliefs and in the rules of their orders, it is difficult to decide.

Philo, who had visited Judea when he was a young man, may have been in actual contact with them. He says they lived in "Syria Palestine" and numbered about four thousand. Originally, he continues, they had dwelt only in villages, avoiding cities, thus implying that at the time he wrote they had removed this restriction and were not limited to the rural areas.

Philo further describes them as abstaining from the sacrifice of animals, "regarding a reverent mind as the only true sacrifice" (which would exclude them from worship at the Temple), engaged in agriculture "and other peaceful arts," and strongly opposed to slavery. They had no time, he continues, for the discussion of abstract questions of philosophy, unless it contributed to ethical teaching. It was moral philosophy with which they were concerned, especially as they discovered it in the Jewish Torah. They kept the Sabbath strictly, meeting in their synagogues, where they were seated in ranks of precedence in accordance with the rules of their order. The scriptures were read by a learned member of the community, who expounded them in a special way "by means of symbols."

The content of the teaching was "piety, holiness, justice, the art of regulating home and city, knowledge of what is really good and bad and of what is indifferent, what ends to avoid, what to pursue—in short, love of God, of virtue, and of man." This teaching bore fruit. The Essenes were widely noted for their kindness, their equality, their indifference to money and to worldly aims and pleasures. They lived in colonies where they had a common storehouse, common vestments, a common treasury into which each placed his earnings and from which expenditures were made on behalf of all. Visitors from other colonies of the sect were warmly received and shared freely in the common meals and religious observances. Even cruel and deceitful tyrants, says Philo, were

* See the Appendix for extended quotations. The reader will find these useful in forming his own judgment on some of the contested points discussed here.

moved to admiration by the Essenes' benevolence and piety.

In his *Praeparatio Evangelica,* Eusebius quotes Philo as saying further that the Essenes inhabited "many cities of Judea, as well as many villages and populous tracts" and that their membership in the sect is from freedom of choice "and not as a matter of race." They do not marry and there are no children in their communities.

From this description, we would suppose that the Essenic movement was widely spread, at least through Judea, and that it consisted of a large number of local communities linked together by common beliefs and practices into what might be called a church. The implication is clear that the movement was not connected with the synagogues of the Pharisees but maintained its own. Although there are indications of asceticism, it seems not to be rigorous, and nowhere are we told that the Essenes were monastics.

When we come to Pliny the Elder, however, we find the Essenes described as "a solitary race" living on the west shore of the Dead Sea. They are "strange above all others in the entire world," living without women, eschewing money, dwelling "among the palm trees." Every day there "flock to them from afar" the disillusioned and world-weary, and thus, although they have no children, their numbers are maintained. This is a description of a monastic settlement, localized in the wilderness, and in fact immediately brings to mind the community at Qumrân. Pliny says the settlement was on the west shore of the Dead Sea, north of Engedi, which narrows down to less than twenty miles the area of its location. Nothing is known of any other monastery within this region that fits Pliny's description.* If, however, it was at Qumrân that the Essenes were established, what of the widespread movement described by Philo?

Perhaps we can answer this question better if first we listen to Josephus. The Essenes arose, he tells us, at the same time as the Sadducees and the Pharisees, namely, during the decline of the Maccabean movement at about the middle of the second century B.C. What the Pharisees had found wrong with the Jerusalem hierarchy, so, evidently, had the Essenes. One of them, named Judas, taught Essenic doctrine in the Temple at the end of the second century, and particularly the art of predicting events. Herod excused the Essenes from taking the oath of loyalty to the crown, such an oath being repugnant to Essenic piety. In Jerusalem, in the first century A.D., there was a Gate of the Essenes at the southeast corner. These are indications of a party of considerable size, influential and widely recognized.

* See Chapter 1, Section 3.

The name *Essenes* was given to the sect, says Josephus, because of its saintliness.* They had no one city but were sojourners in many cities. They did not marry, but adopted the children of others, training them in Essenic doctrine and practice. There was another sect, however, also counted Essenic, in which marriage was permitted where women had proved their devoutness for three trial years. There was no private ownership of property. Wealth was surrendered, as also were the daily earnings, to a common fund, which was administered by stewards on behalf of the community. In every city there was a special officer who took care of vestments and supplies and provided for traveling members. It was an Essenic duty to assist the poor and needy, irrespective of whether or not they belonged to the Essenic party.

Josephus likens the Essenes to the Pythagoreans, a semi-religious order founded by Pythagoras, Greek philosopher and mathematician, in 520 B.C. thus suggesting Hellenic influence. The Essenes may also be likened to the Therapeutae of Alexandria, who, however, were more given to mysticism and contemplation. The question of the possible extent to which Greek ideas entered into Essenic thinking has often been discussed but with no very certain conclusions. It is known from the books of the Maccabees that kinship had been claimed between the Spartans and the Jews as far back as 309 B.C., when Areus, king of Sparta, had written to the high priest, Onias, that "It is found in writing that the Spartans and the Jews are brethren, and that they are of the stock of Abraham" (I Mac. xii, 21). Again in 144 B.C., the high priest Jonathan reminded the Spartans that the long-standing friendship between Spartans and Jews was based on ancient kinship. This is certainly astonishing information, but it must not for that reason be set aside. Possibly, the Hellenizing party among the Jews desired to establish a reference point, however mythical, to foster close ties in Judaic and Greek relations.

A curious element of Essenic ritual, according to Josephus, was worship of the sun, to which they prayed at dawn. This practice was probably adopted from Zoroastrian or Mithraic religion. Other elements in Essenic doctrine, as, for instance, the belief in angels, undoubtedly come from Persia and were probably absorbed during the Exile.

After the prayer to the sun at daybreak, the Essenes, Jose-

---

*In Greek, ὁσιότητα, from ὁσιόω, to make holy; ὅσιος, however, means approved by natural law, not ἱερός, sacred (to the gods), nor yet δίκαιος established by human law (teaching). As far as the Greek is concerned, therefore (and it is from the Greek that the word Essene is derived), we have the idea not only of a hallowed way of life but of a way of life commanded by natural law.

phus tells us, were sent away by their superintendents to their appointed work, according to the arts in which they were skilled, and in this they remained employed until the fifth hour (11 A.M.). They then assembled in one place, clothed themselves in white vestments, and bathed in cold water. This sacrament of purification being completed, they entered the exclusive refectory into which no one not of their order was ever admitted, and partook of a common meal presided over by a priest. This was followed by the singing of thanksgiving psalms, after which the sacred vestments were set aside and they returned to their work. At the end of the day, the evening meal was solemnized with similar observances, no one being given more to eat than the minimum that would sustain him.

To join the sect, it was necessary to serve a novitiate of one year, subject to all the disciplines of the order but without being admitted to its privileges. At the end of this period, if the novice had given proof of his worthiness he was permitted to share more closely in the sectarian way of life and to use a more sacred "water of purification." After two years, if admitted, he took "tremendous oaths": 1) to reverence God; 2) to be just towards men; 3) to hate the wicked. Other oaths were to respect those in authority, to exercise authority justly if he, himself, were vested with it, to wear simple clothing, to love truth and abjure falsehood, to abstain from all unholy gain, to conceal nothing from members of the order, to communicate the doctrine of the sect only as he had received it, to preserve the scriptures of the sect and never to reveal the names of the angels (used perhaps in incantations?).

In addition, the name of Moses must be reverenced next to that of Jehovah. Death was the penalty for "blaspheming against Moses." We see from this how intensely Jewish the sect was, and yet they also accepted the non-Jewish belief in immortality of the soul. The typical Jewish expectation had been concerned with all Israel and its characteristic context was terrestrial; the Essenes, however, to quote Josephus, "in agreement with the opinions of the Greeks, declare that there lies away across the ocean a habitation for the good souls . . . but they allot to the bad souls a dark and tempestuous den full of never-ceasing punishments."

It will be noted that Josephus' description of the Essenes, at least as to the details of the ritual, would apply better to a monastic sect, such as Pliny tells us was located near the Dead Sea, than it would to a widespread movement with branches in many cities. The daily baptism of a considerable group by immersion in sanctified water would seem to be more feasible where elaborate arrangements could be made for it, as at the monastery, than under conditions prevailing in cities where water was not plentiful but must usually be taken from springs or drawn from wells and carried to the points where it was used.

Nevertheless, it is clear that Josephus knew the Essenes as a widespread movement, a party that had, as he says, no single city. The only reasonable explanation is that Essenic sects, perhaps within a total party which was loosely called the Essenes (the "holy ones," the "saints"), exhibited considerable variety in their practices, as they may also have done in their doctrines. With this view in mind, we shall examine the relation of the Essenes to the sect of the Dead Sea Scrolls.

8. *The Essenes and the Sect of the Scrolls*

The scroll from the 1947 cave which tells us something of the rules and ritual of the Qumrân community is the Manual of Discipline. It is by no means a complete compilation, and there is much that we would like to know of which there is no mention. Nevertheless, it is impossible to read it without being immediately struck by the marked similarities between the provisions of this document and those of the Essenes as described by Josephus. If the Qumrân community was not a settlement of the Essenes themselves, it was at least *Essenic*. One could easily imagine that if the Essenic party was a widespread movement, this monastery on the shores of the Dead Sea was its headquarters, the heart and center of its corporate life. One could equally imagine that the movement began here. It is possible. And yet, we must proceed cautiously: we do not know. There are considerations to the contrary.

Besides the Manual of Discipline, there is another document that deals with the rules of an Essenic order, though less completely even than the Manual. This is the famous Damascus Document, to which we have previously made reference but which we must now more particularly describe.

The Damascus Document was discovered early in the present century in a *genizah* at Cairo, and was published by Solomon Schechter in 1910. The title given to it when it was presented to Cambridge University was "Fragments of a Zadokite Work." This was because the sect that wrote and used it claimed to be the true Zadokites (spiritual descendants of Zadok, who, it will again be remembered, was one of the high priests of David, appointed by Solomon to be the first high priest of the new Jerusalem temple) in distinction, apparently, from the Sadducees, the false Zadokites who had debased the priestly office under Hasmonean rule in the second century.

The fragments are from two manuscripts which largely duplicate each other (there are a number of minor differences) and which are therefore thought of in combination and referred to as though they formed one document. Prominent

features of the document are the reference to a flight to Damascus to escape persecution and mention of a "new covenant" which was made in Damascus between the sect and
Jehovah. These important facts have caused it to be known
as the *Damaskusschrift,* or Damascus Document.

Until the finding of the Scrolls, the Damascus Document
was very difficult to date, its period of composition being the
subject of much controversy. But now that fragments of a
copy of it have been found in the Qumrân caves, we know
that it is at least as early as the latest of the Scrolls. Almost
certainly it is later than the Isaiah Scroll, but we do not know
whether it is later or earlier than the Manual of Discipline. Its
precise date, however, is of less importance than that it was
one of the books in the library at Qumrân.[19]

The similarity between parts of the Damascus Document
and the Manual of Discipline are so close that the two must
come from the same source or from related sources within the
same movement. In the Manual, those who are passing into
the order are required to say, "We have committed iniquity,
we have transgressed, we have sinned, we have done evil, we
and our fathers before us, in walking contrary to the statutes
of truth." In the Damascus Document, the rendering is, "We
have sinned, we have done wickedly, both we and our fathers,
in walking contrary to the statutes of the covenant." Equally
close similarities are immediately perceivable throughout this
section. Where the one manuscript says "guilty heart," the
other says "guilty impulse"; where one refers to the "sons of
Israel," the other refers to "the people." Clearly, the two documents contain two versions of the same original text; or perhaps one of them revises the other. This is so in some sections,
but in others the relationship, although identifiable, is general
rather than particular.

It must be noted, however, that the differences are significant
as well as the similarities. Where the Manual says "statutes of
truth," the Damascus Document says "statutes of the covenant." Such differences, if they can be interpreted, may inform
us of changes of thought between one time and another, or
perhaps of variations between the sects within a single party.

In the Damascus Document and the Manual, a number of
provisions are more fully described than they are by Josephus.
There are directions for the appointment of "judges of the congregation," rules concerning purification with water, the Sabbath, the duties of the superintendent, taking decisions in open
meeting, rules of precedence, and rules for examining the
candidate who has served his first novitiate of one year. In
the Manual, there are directions for the appointment of twelve
men and three priests "who are perfect in all that has been
revealed of the whole law," and many other "regulations of

the way for the wise man in these times."

The Essenic sacred meal, described by Josephus, is here pictured for us more fully. Wherever there are ten men of the sect present, "there shall not be absent from them a priest." According to their rank in the order, the members of the community shall "sit before" the priest and shall be asked for their counsel. Then, the table being set with bread and wine, the priest "shall stretch forth his hand first to pronounce a blessing with the first portion of the bread and wine."

There are restrictions concerning those who "shall enter the water," obviously referring to the daily immersions reported by Josephus and provided for at the monastery at Qumrân. There are rules for contributing wealth to the general treasury, rules against speaking in anger, rules requiring the lesser to obey the greater. However, no mention is made of the dietary requirements and strict regulation of work hours reported by Josephus. There are also other features of Essenic life which, if Josephus' description is to be the criterion, are either missing or seem differently represented in this Scroll.

This has given rise to the question as to whether Josephus was entirely accurate. These documents, it is contended, carry us directly into Essenic life, whereas Josephus only describes it at second hand. This argument is not untenable. However, it substitutes the Qumrân community for Josephus as a criterion and obliges us to ask what sect Josephus was describing.

Josephus called it the Essenes. Nowhere in the Scrolls does the community give itself this name—or indeed any other specific name—but only general designations. But as to this, it may be that the Essenes never used this name themselves. They may not have wished to call themselves "the holy ones." It may have been what they were called by others.

However, it is impossible to believe that Josephus was not describing—and on the whole correctly—a movement that had branches in many cities. It is impossible to reject the testimony of Philo that the movement had "colonies" throughout Judea. Both were reporting as contemporaries. Though their books may have been published after the Essenes were dispersed (70 A.D.), the writers had lived while the sect was still flourishing. It is true that in characterizing the Sadducees and Pharisees, Josephus wields a deft pen; but he leaves them still recognizable. If he has done anything similar in the case of the Essenes—as, for example, if he has made them seem more Hellenic than they actually were—this is no reason for believing that his account of their rules and ritual is not in the main accurate or that he was mistaken in saying that the movement was not merely local. Josephus had traveled widely; he was a general of the Jewish forces during the war of 67–70 A.D. We must, in the main, accept his description.

The same is true of Philo. The Essenic movement, as he knew of it (and may have observed it), was a religious party or church with branches in rural areas and in many cities. On the whole, he corroborates Josephus. The Damascus Document also implies the existence of local groups. The best we can do, of course, is to evaluate the testimony available to us. We do not have all the Scrolls of the Qumrân monastery. We do not know how much of the evidence that is missing would be supplied by writings which have not been found. We must go on the basis of the knowledge that we possess and the evidence that we may reasonably believe.

On this basis, we may conclude that the Essenic party was widely distributed in the Palestine of the first century A.D., but that its main features, as we had knowledge of them prior to the discovery of the Scrolls, are so much in accord with those of the Manual of Discipline and the Damascus Document that, in spite of discrepancies, we are compelled to see a close relationship between the sect of the Scrolls and the Essenic party. This is confirmed by the testimony of Pliny the Elder, who spoke of a settlement of Essenes in the very area in which the Qumrân monastery was located. *The community of Qumrân was thus an Essenic community;* this we cannot doubt, *but its relationship to the rest of the movement can only be conjectured.*

Because of such facts as its location not far from Jerusalem, the size of its library, the impressive baptistries, the scriptorium, the large cemetery, it is an inevitable conjecture that the monastery was the headquarters of the entire movement. But it must at the same time be admitted that the Essenic party, whether its headquarters were at Qumrân or not, almost certainly contained divisions or sects varying from one another in rules and ritual—and perhaps in doctrine—and it may also be assumed that these sects were not static during the party's more than two centuries of existence, but were constantly changing and developing.

This fact of change and variety within the Essenic party, while it complicates the question of identity and increases our perplexities, may well be significant for the rise of Christianity. Some of the Essenes may have changed comparatively little; but others may have changed enough to make them the inevitable nucleus of the Christian movement. But to this we shall come in its own place.

9. Essenic Beliefs and the Teacher of Righteousness

As we have now seen, the Jewish religious party with which the Qumrân sect was connected—and which it may have created—must be viewed as a movement whose development, like that of all other movements known to history, produced changes and variations. If we regard the Qumrân monastics as the norm, Essenic belief and practice in other places may have differed from it considerably. Since, however, there is every likelihood that the Dead Sea Sect, which had chosen the wilderness rather than cities for its habitation, was ruggedly clinging to the more rigorous rules of the order, striving thus to maintain its doctrines and its pieties undiluted, its scriptures are the surest sources that we have for understanding what was at the heart of the entire movement.

What, according to these scriptures, did the monastics of Qumrân believe? First and foremost, they believed that they belonged to a chosen people, the people of the first covenant and of the Law of Moses, and that Jehovah had called them to be an "elect" among this people, "returning" to the Law of Moses and fulfilling it in every way. So sacred was the Law of Moses that, according to the Damascus Document, it could not be mentioned in an oath. Sinai was not merely a turning point in history but a cosmic intervention through which Jehovah had made an everlasting covenant with the Children of Israel, the provisions of which must be sacredly honored and solemnly obeyed. This obligation, the priests and rulers of Israel had shamefully betrayed. The monastics, although condemning this betrayal, must also "redeem" it by their own faithfulness. It was thus their constant study to understand the Mosaic Law precisely and obey it literally.

Second, they believed that Jehovah had consolidated his promise in the reign of David, his "Anointed One." David's victories were the foreshadowing of the final triumph of Israel. David himself was the Sacred King of whose lineage the "Anointed One" that was to come would be derived. With David stood Zadok, the first and holiest of the high priests of Jerusalem. The priests of the monastics were "descended" from Zadok, the true Zadokites who had followed righteousness, and were sharply at variance with the evil Zadokites (Sadducees) who were profaning Jehovah's altars, amassing unrighteous wealth, making wars of spoliation to steal the fruits which came from the labors of the needy. Whether all the priests of the sect were "Levites" as well as Zadokites or precisely how priests were selected is not clear; the relationship of the priesthood to Aaron, the brother of Moses, who was the first Jehovistic priest, is also not plain. But Aaron was certainly regarded as an exalted figure, and whether literally or in symbolism, was closely connected with the "Anointed One" (or "Ones": more than one Messiah may have been expected) who was eagerly awaited.

Third, they believed in a prophet to come, either Elijah or

patterned upon Elijah. This was in any case a widespread Jewish anticipation and had been so for some time. When Judas Maccabeus tore down the defiled altar of the Temple upon which Antiochus Epiphanes had offered swine-flesh, he did not know in such unprecedented circumstances what it was ritually appropriate to do with the polluted stones and so ordered them laid up "till a prophet should rise to say what should be done with them." There are many other references to decisions which must await this prophet, although his chief function, as it came to be defined, was that of preceding and preparing the way for the "Anointed One."

Fourth, the Qumrân community was deeply imbued with the spirit of the prophets, the Amos who said "Let justice roll down like waters," the Isaiah and Jeremiah who had promised that Jehovah would bring salvation when his people returned to righteousness. All of the "written" prophets are represented, it is believed, in the fragments recovered from the caves; and, of course, two of the Scrolls are of the book of Isaiah. It is from the prophets that the great ethical impulse came which moved the sectarians to justice and benevolence in their relations with each other and towards the righteous outside their community. The "evil ones" they felt bound to hate, and this, too, we must acknowledge, can be supported from the prophets, for Jehovah was depicted as a God of wrath when his will was not obeyed.

It must also be remembered that it was the prophetic movement that had produced the book of Deuteronomy, which the monastics regarded as a book of Moses. The prophetic message was therefore represented in the Law as well as in the books that the prophets had written.

Fifth, it is clear that the Essenic movement had joined in a "New Covenant" (which, it may be noted, is synonymous with "New Testament"), apparently at Damascus. Or, if the entire party was not included in this particular enactment of the new covenant, the sect that wrote the Damascus Document most certainly was. In any case, it is a covenant to return to the Law of Moses, guided, however, by a Teacher of Righteousness, "the priest into whose heart God put wisdom to explain all the words of his servants, the prophets," and who also had predicted "all the things that are coming upon his people and his congregation."

The Teacher of Righteousness, to whom the sect ascribed such extraordinary authority, was first introduced to the modern world when the Damascus Document was published (1910). In this document he is called both a "Teacher of Righteousness" and a "Unique Teacher," and there is a further reference to one "who shall teach righteousness at the ending of days." When the Habakkuk Scroll was published, it was at once noticed that there are no less than seven direct references to a Teacher of Righteousness as well as a reference to a priest "into whose heart God gave wisdom" so that he possessed a foreknowledge of the future."

Who was this Teacher of Righteousness?[20] Unfortunately, there is no sure way of identifying him, and the attempt to do so has led to considerable controversy. Scholars have contended that the question hinges upon the answers to two other questions: Who were the *Kittim*? And what historical personalities of the second and first centuries B.C. fit the description of the Teacher and his persecutors, the Wicked Priest and the Man of the Lie?

The word *Kittim*,* which may have meant originally the Greek and Latin peoples from the Mediterranean islands, came to be applied to any dominant military power from the west, and the mention of the Kittim in the Habakkuk Scroll may therefore be interpreted as meaning the Seleucids, who were Greeks, or the later invading Romans. If the former were intended, the Scroll relates to the second century B.C., and if the latter, to the first century. The date of the Teacher of Righteousness would thus be fixed in either one century or the other if we could know who the Kittim were. At the time of this writing, the question has not been settled, but the weight of opinion is in the direction of the Romans.[21]

Another possible clue in identifying the Teacher of Righteousness would be any strong indication as to who the Wicked Priest and the Man of the Lie might have been. Among the dramatis personae of the second and first centuries B.C., the available figures to fill these roles (or role: the Wicked Priest and the Man of the Lie could have been one person) are extraordinarily numerous. It is almost incredible that so many unconscionable rascals should have occupied positions of power within so short a period.

When it comes to the possible candidates for the role of the Teacher of Righteousness, the field is much sparser. Onias III, the high priest deposed and banished by Antiochus Epiphanes, has been suggested, in which case his rival, Menelaus, who persecuted him, would be the Wicked Priest. If Aristobulus I, of the turn of the century, is adopted as the Wicked Priest, the Teacher of Righteousness might have been Judah the Essene, whom Josephus describes as having taught at the Temple, instructing his disciples in divining the future. If, however, Judas had so prominent a role in history, why does Josephus

---

* Hebrew: כתים, (pronunciation approximately khit-tēēm with stress on second syllable); in King James Bible, Chittim.

say no more about him? Or was he prominent only in the annals of the Essenes?

One of the most persuasive of the theories is that the Teacher of Righteousness was Onias the Righteous, who, according to Josephus, was stoned to death in 65 B.C. In this case, the leader of the Sadducees could be called the Wicked Priest and the leader of the Pharisees the Man of the Lie, since both parties were opposed to Onias and both seem to have blamed his martyrdom on the other.

It must be admitted that the problem of identification is difficult and elusive, and also extremely technical. The general reader will find the utmost difficulty in following the theories advanced by the various scholars, although he may admire the skill with which they demolish each other's hypotheses. The truth is that, at least at the time these words are written, there is no conclusive way of identifying the Teacher of Righteousness.

Did he then exist? It cannot seriously be doubted. The fact that there is no account of him by secular historians is no more impressive in his case than in that of Jesus. Was Jesus himself the Teacher of Righteousness? The possibility has been considered but has had to be discarded; the Teacher and Jesus are separated by at least a century.

What we can be reasonably sure of is that the Teacher of Righteousness was a priest, perhaps a high priest of the Temple, who lived in either the second or first century B.C., probably the latter, and who led his followers into a new Mosaic covenant, forming them into a religious order, instructing them in the meaning of the scriptures, adding his own teaching and his prophecies, and remaining the martyred prophet of the order, adored and venerated and expected to play a part in the Messianic age of the future.

At this point, it should be remarked that we might know a great deal more about all these matters if a copy were found —or even sizable fragments—of the book "HGW" which is mentioned in the Damascus Document and the Manual of Discipline as a text of high value. This mysterious missing scroll has aroused much speculation and appears to be the key which—if we had it—would unlock the door to some of the secrets that still tantalize us.

A further belief of the convenanters of Qumrân, and one of the highest importance, was that Jehovah would send his "Anointed"—or Messiah—to end the existing world order and inaugurate a new one. The expectation of a Messiah* was

---

* Hebrew: משׁיח translated into Greek as Χριστος; in English as Christ. Christ is not the name of a person but of an office, the office of the "Anointed." Literally, any "anointed one" was a Χριστος or Christ. The reader must beware of attaching this name

widely held and not limited to our covenanters. The latter, however, had their own special view of Messiahship. In the Manual of Discipline, we read of "the coming of a prophet and the Anointed Ones of Aaron and Israel." In the Damascus Document, it appears that there is only one Messiah: "the Anointed One of Aaron and Israel." The Messiah of Aaron would be a priestly Messiah, in accordance with the sacerdotal tradition, while the Messiah of Israel would be the "Anointed One" of the lineage of David. It is possible that as the thinking of the sect progressed, the two Messiahs were merged into one.

Dupont-Sommer is sure that this is what took place.[22] He also argues, and persuasively, that the expected Messiah was identical with the Teacher of Righteousness. Although this can by no means be demonstrated beyond argument, it has so much inherent probability that it deserves much consideration. The objection to it, based on the text itself, is that the most pertinent passage in the Damascus Document reads as follows: "From the day when the unique Teacher was carried away until the coming of the Anointed of Aaron and Israel." The Teacher and the Anointed seem thus to be regarded as separate persons. But, says Dupont-Sommer, the use of two phrases to characterize the same person acting in two distinct capacities "is a feature of the most elementary rhetoric. It is all the better justified here," he continues, "by each of the two expressions being very well chosen; when the death of the great righteous man is referred to, the author employs the expression 'Teacher of Righteousness,' which suits his earthly career better. When, on the other hand, the ultimate coming is referred to, he gives him the title of 'the Anointed,' since this coming is, as it were, the flowering of the Messianic character [career]."[23]

That this is a natural interpretation seems to Dupont-Sommer the more likely since, before the discovery of the Scrolls, Solomon Schechter, who first translated and published the Damascus Document, held the same view. "The only Teacher, or Teacher of Righteousness," wrote Schechter, "is identical with mâshiah [Messiah] . . . whose advent is expected by the sect."

There is also the fact that in the Habakkuk Scroll there is a reference to the faithful being redeemed by God because of their "faith in the Teacher of Righteousness." One is inevitably reminded, in all these respects, of the parallel situa-

---

to Jesus in the present context. It could be applied to David or Zadok, "Anointed Ones" of the past, or to an unnamed "Anointed" of the future.

tion in the case of Jesus. When thinking of him as a teacher in Galilee, his followers would naturally refer to him as Jesus. But when he was the expected "Anointed One," they referred to him as "Christ." The Gospels, in fact, do call him Jesus when speaking of his ministry; but the Acts and the Epistles, which are concerned with the period after his death, refer to him as "the Lord Jesus" or "Christ Jesus" or "the Lord Jesus Christ."

Other beliefs of the covenanters have been seen by scholars to bear a marked resemblance to Gnosticism, traditionally regarded as a Christian heresy of the early centuries but which must now be seen to have been Judaic, thus exemplifying the gradual transition from "heretical" Judaism to "heretical" Christianity. Gnosticism's principal tenet was that a divine Redeemer (Teacher of Righteousness?) had come to earth to implant in men a mystical saving knowledge, which is similar to the covenanters' belief that they had a special kind of knowledge which illumined their understanding of the divine plan and the path to salvation.

The monastics, like other Essenes, were evidently fatalists in part. God had predestined at least the main direction and the chief events of history, and had willed long in advance its final consummation. There was a war, as there had been from the beginning, between the "Sons of Light" and the "Sons of Darkness." It was a struggle, as St. Paul was a little later to express it, "not against flesh and blood, but against principalities, against the powers, against the world-rulers of this darkness, against the spiritual hosts of wickedness in the heavenly places" (Eph. vi, 12). This came from Zoroastrianism, illustrating the powerful influence of Persian religion, first upon Judaism, then upon the Judaic Messianic religion which eventually became Christianity.[24] The Scroll describing "The War of the Sons of Light with the Sons of Darkness," although no doubt Judaically eschatological, is also imbued with the Persian conception.

A further belief has only recently been discerned, but it is of the utmost importance, not only for our understanding of the covenanters but because of what its currency may signify for the Messianic consciousness of Jesus. A passage in Isaiah,* probably from the second century B.C., has long been connected with the Redeemership of Jesus. This is historically impossible (although, of course, dogmatically it can be affirmed), and scholars have seen in it an interpretation of the

* The book of Isaiah comes only in part from the eighth century B.C. prophet of that name. What we have is in fact three books: 1) chaps. 1–35; 2) 36–39; 3) 40–66. Even of the first section, only part can be considered the authentic prophecies of Isaiah himself.

role to be played by the Jewish nation itself rather than by an individual. On any rendering, the passage is obscure. At the same time, it is extremely moving and must always have been influential.

This passage, the fifty-third chapter, describes one who was "despised and rejected of men, a man of sorrows and acquainted with grief: and as one from whom men hide their face he was despised, and we esteemed him not. Surely he hath borne our griefs and carried our sorrows . . . and Jehovah hath laid on him the iniquity of us all" (RV).[25]

Brownlee, in retranslating parts of the Manual of Discipline,[26] points out that the *raison-d'être* itself of the Qumrân community was to follow out the exhortation in Isaiah to "prepare in the wilderness the way of Jehovah, make straight in the desert a highway for our God"; and that the community came to see itself in the role of the "Servant of the Lord" of Isaiah 53. The most pertinent passage in the Manual is as follows:

When these things come to pass in Israel, the Council of the Community will have been established in truth: As an external planting ["my planting, the work of my hands," Isa. 1x, 21; "that they might be called trees of righteousness, the planting of Jehovah," Isa. lxi, 3], a holy house of Israel, a most holy institution of Aaron, . . . to make atonement for the earth, and to decree the condemnation of wickedness that there may be no more perversity (IQS, viii, 5-10).

Interpreting the closing psalm of the Manual, Brownlee sees the threefold function of the Servant of Jehovah, with which the community had identified itself, as witness (prophetic), atonement (priestly), and judgment (kingly). The realization of this function must be largely through the community itself, but supremely it could be achieved only by the Teacher of Righteousness.

It is only a step from this to the Teacher of Righteousness as the Messiah who is "Prophet, Priest and King." The spiritual lineage of Moses and the prophets, of Aaron, Zadok and the high priests, of David and the "anointed" kings of Israel and Judah, all merge to produce one "Anointed One" who is to bring on the Kingdom of God through his sufferings. The conception may not have been as fully developed as this when the Manual was written, but if it was moving in this direction why should the development not have been complete by the time Jesus could have encountered it?

The further beliefs of the covenanters must be left to fuller treatments and the gradual clarification of meanings and exegesis. But before closing this section, let us remind ourselves once more that the covenanters, as they viewed themselves, were living at the center of history, prime movers in the drama

of a saga soon to be concluded. To the modern mind, such an
extreme projection of a national dilemma into historical and
cosmic phenomenology seems incredibly ethnomanic and morbid. But it is necessary to see that the driving forces behind it
all were guilt and sin and what were seen to be their dreadful
consequences. God could not save even his chosen people if
they would not heed his call to righteousness.

The world was evil. Its greeds and lusts were leering everywhere, mocking the God of all creation. That such a world
should be destroyed seemed obvious. That its destruction was
imminent could nowhere be more easily imagined than on the
shores of the Dead Sea. Thirteen hundred feet below the level
of the Mediterranean, between a lake of "imprisoned, bitter
waters," and desolate cliffs, "bare, unbroken, menacing," there
are few places in the world, says George Adam Smith, in his
classical description, "where the sun beats with so fierce a
heat. In this awful hollow, this bit of the infernal regions
come up to the surface, this hell with the sun shining into it,
primitive man laid the scene of God's most terrible judgment
on human sin."[27]

He refers, of course, to Sodom and Gomorrah* and the fire
that rained from heaven. That a cataclysm occurred need not
be doubted. The Dead Sea was once called the Lake of
Asphalt. Bitumen is abundant. There are large petroleum de-
posits. The geological story of the Dead Sea and the Gohr
above it, through which the Jordan wends its melancholy way,
is itself a saga. Great movements of the earth's crust in the
primordial epoch were followed in later ages by mighty
earthquakes. Fierce thunderstorms hurled bolts of lightning
from the sky. All that was necessary was the coincidence of
an earthquake, throwing up thousands of tons of petroleum,
with an electrical storm to ignite the gushing floods of oil.
Even the "brimstone" is abundant. Many of the springs that
flow into the Dead Sea are strongly sulphurous to this day.

Here on the shores of the Lake Asphaltitis, as in the time
of the covenanters it was called, stood our Qumrân monastery. "Perhaps there is no region of our earth," says George
Adam Smith, "where Nature and History have more cruelly
conspired, where so tragic a drama has obtained so awful
a theatre. . . . The history of the Dead Sea opens with Sodom
and Gomorrah and may be said to close with the Massacre
of Masada."[28]

Between these two events, however, and for a time, the wilderness a few miles south, at Engedi, had been made to "blos-
som as the rose." Irrigation had created an ephemeral paradise

---

* The Arabs insist that Qumrân is the site of Gomorrah. In
Arabic, the pronunciations are alike.

in the midst of the eternal desert. Our monastics knew of it and believed that in other ways, too, the wilderness could be changed into a fertile field. After the evil time, with the coming of the "Anointed One"—when "the crooked shall be made straight and the rough places plain" and all flesh could see "the salvation of God"—then, even here on the dreary, barren shores of the Dead Sea, "upon the banks thereof, on this side and on that side, shall come up all trees for food, whose leaf shall not fade, neither shall the fruit thereof be consumed . . . because the waters thereof issue forth from the Sanctuary" (Ezek. xlvii, 12).

So our covenanters believed, while they battled for Jehovah, awaiting his "Anointed One," as prophesied by their Teacher of Righteousness.

10. *What Happened to the Essenes?*

The Roman occupation of Judea was for a while fairly quiet. Roman rulers were in many ways as just as they were rapacious, and, in any case, they were scarcely greedier than the native kings. Antigonus, the last of the Maccabean line, was succeeded in 37 B.C. by Herod who was called the Great. Herod built many splendid buildings, founded the seaport of Caesarea, and began the restoration of the Temple, which, however, was not completed until 64 A.D., six years before it was again destroyed. When he died in 4 B.C., there were few who sincerely mourned him.

After Herod, the kingdom was divided. Antipas, who ruled in Galilee, married his brother's wife and was rebuked by John the Baptist, whom he executed. When he was defeated in battle by Aretas, the father of his first wife whom he had put away, the people regarded it as a punishment for decapitating John. He ruled until 34 A.D.

In Judea, Archelaus reigned for ten years until 6 A.D., but his rule was so bad that Augustus removed him and turned Judea into a Roman province under a procurator of low rank who reported to the Governor of Syria. One of the procurators was Pontius Pilatus, who held this office from 26 to 36 A.D., after which he was recalled and banished to Gaul.

The tension between the Jewish people and their Roman rulers gradually increased. The Romans were not able to understand what looked to them like demented religious fanaticism, and the Jews were not able to tolerate what they counted sacrilege. Jew was disdainful of Roman, Roman was contemptuous of Jew. Pilatus was bewildered and outraged at the resistance of the Jews to the Roman military ensigns being brought into Jerusalem. It was done elsewhere as a matter of routine; why not in Judea? For the charge of idolatry, he had neither comprehension nor patience. But since his choice was between retreat and more bloodshed than he cared to report to Rome, he retreated.

The Emperor Caligula directed that his statue be set up in the Jerusalem Temple. Beseeched by Herod Agrippa, he rescinded the order but would probably have reissued it if, in the meanwhile, he had not been assassinated. Agrippa, who died in 44 A.D., was the last king of the Jews. After that, all Palestine was under direct Roman rule. Because of the frequent recourse of the governor, Antonius Felix, to mass crucifixions, there arose a sect called the Sicarii, who made life in Jerusalem hazardous for all Romans by their skill in assassination. Felix did what he could to suppress the Sicarii, but also employed them to murder the high priest Jonathan who had been a moderating influence and whose death was a tragic loss. Porcius Festus succeeded Felix but died after two years.

During this time, what was happening at Qumrân and to the Essenic party generally, we do not know. But we do know that what came to be known as the Christian movement had by now developed, and that it was similar in many of its doctrines, as it was in its sacraments and its organization, to the Essenic sects and to the "new covenanters" at Qumrân. The Christians may not as yet (62 A.D.) have been generally known by that name; more usually, they were known as the sect of the Nazarenes. But to this we shall come in the next chapter, noting only in the present summary that after the death of Festus, and before a new governor could arrive, the high priest Ananus seized the opportunity to assassinate James, the brother of Jesus and head of the Nazarene movement, for which Ananus was deposed by Agrippa II.

Judean affairs by now were not only bad; they had reached the point of social dissolution. Brigandage was rife; no one remained in jail who could afford the bribe that bought his release. Responsible government was at an end. Gessius Florus, who "ruled" from 64 to 66 A.D., proceeded from routine murder to frequent massacre, and at last was driven by the populace from Jerusalem, where the Roman garrison surrendered but was nevertheless put to death. This was rebellion and the signal for war.

The Christians, who by this time saw little to choose between the Romans and the Sadducean priests, fled from Judea across the Jordan, taking no part in the Jewish revolt. It is said that there were Essenes who also would not fight, but whether the two groups were connected we can only speculate. That there were Essenes who did fight, at least in this revolt, has frequently been asserted, but the testimony upon which the assertion is chiefly based, that of Josephus, speaks only of valiantly suffering torture.[29]

To meet the crisis, the Jews formed an emergency government and placed Josephus—destined to achieve greater fame as an historian than as a soldier—in charge of the defense of Galilee. He fought stoutly but was defeated and went over to the Romans. The Pharisees, who had controlled the emergency government down to now, and who had tried to invoke a policy of moderation, were brushed aside. Josephus was a Pharisee and was believed to have been halfhearted in the struggle. He had now gone over to the enemy. Angrily, the reckless Zealots took over and moderation was at an end.

If Israel had been united and less eaten away by corruption, the war need not have been a hopeless one. But as it was, it could end in only one way. Jerusalem was torn by factional strife; Jews massacred Jews and the slaughter rivaled all the butcheries of the Romans. In the late summer of 70 A.D., the outer court of the Temple was set afire, but the fighting went on even around the altar of burnt offering. At last, it was all over; the site where Zadok had stood to offer sacrifice, and upon which one temple after another had been erected, was left, as Jesus had predicted that it would be, with "not one stone upon another."

As calamity followed calamity, the Qumrân monastics may well have believed that the "Day of Jehovah" had at last arrived and that the Messiah for whom they had waited would immediately appear. The moon, it was true, had not yet "turned into blood," nor had the stars fallen from the sky, but destruction had come to the "evil ones" who had ruled in Israel, and it was time now for Jehovah to turn his hand against the Kittim.

Perhaps they waited until almost the last moment. But they knew the Romans would come. They put their precious manuscripts into the jars prepared for them, and climbed laboriously up to the caves. Here, the Romans would never think to search. Some day, perhaps, when the fighting was over, the covenanters would come back. Perhaps they thought it would be soon. Surely the time was near! God could not wait! Not now! The new age must begin! The time had come! The "Sons of Belial" had had their day. Jehovah must fulfill his promise: his faithful would not doubt it. . . . And when they returned, their scriptures still would be their treasure—perhaps more so than ever—when the Messiah of Aaron and of Israel presided over their sacred meal, in the Day of the Lord Jehovah, and of the Kingdom that came from God.

4

The Scrolls and Christian Origins

1. The Scholars and the Laity

In an earlier chapter, we quoted the opinion of W. F. Albright that the discovery of the Scrolls had produced "new evidence with regard to the beliefs and practices of Jewish sectarians of the last two centuries B.C." that "bids fair to revolutionize our approach to the beginnings of Christianity." We mentioned also Dupont-Sommer's statement that "all the problems relative to primitive Christianity henceforth find themselves placed in a new light, which forces us to reconsider them completely."*

New Testament scholars in the United States, as Edmund Wilson noted, were for several years strongly reluctant to take these opinions seriously. Latterly, however, as we saw in the same earlier chapter, New Testament scholars, prodded by Mr. Wilson and the extraordinary public interest that was taken in the Scrolls, have broken their silence. But few of them have been willing to agree that the Scrolls mean anything revolutionary. They have been excited by the discovery; they have said that it means that we shall now know the background of the New Testament writings better than we did in the past;

* Chapter 1, Section 6.

but they have concluded by saying that no important previous assumptions—and no major articles of orthodox belief—need be revised.

Even Millar Burrows, who is no ordinary scholar but a distinguished Semitic specialist who has worked on the Scrolls almost from the beginning, tells us that "after studying the Dead Sea Scrolls for seven years, I do not find my understanding of the New Testament substantially affected. Its Jewish background is clearer and better understood, but its meaning has neither been changed nor significantly clarified." And he goes on to say that perhaps he "simply cannot see what is" before his eyes. "When visiting archeological excavations," he interestingly informs us, he has sometimes been "unable, with the utmost good will, to see things pointed out by the excavators. It is true," he concludes, "that a trained eye can often see what is invisible to the uninitiated. It is also true that scholars, being human, sometimes fail to distinguish between trained perception and uncritical imagination."[1]

This last sentence is a little ambiguous; it sounds less like self-doubt than a suavely couched reproach to other scholars. In any case, let the layman be warned not to be intimidated. Even the best authorities, when they move out of their fields of technical proficiency (as also no doubt, in varying degrees within them), are not free from subjective pressures, including, of course, those of which they are unconscious. Scholars who can banish all bias when assembling the fragments of ancient manuscripts may not be free from preconceptions when it comes to evaluating what they have assembled.

Interpreters of every sort, especially in matters of religion, should be alertly watched, and this writer is well aware—and fully willing—that this be applied to himself. His aim in what follows will be, first, to present examples of the information familiar to scholars but not usually known to laymen, in the absence of which it is impossible to arrive at an informed judgment; and second, to suggest some new hypotheses, but without protagonistic zeal, and entirely without anxiety for the outcome. Whether sustained or not, such hypotheses will serve their purpose. For the intention is not to convince the reader of particular answers to the thorny questions that the new discovery has raised, but to help him see the true significance of the questions.

First, it must be understood that when the theological scholar* reassures the layman about the implications of the

---

* We prefer to use the broader term, "theological scholars," rather than the narrower one, "New Testament scholars," used in quoting Mr. Wilson and others. "New Testament scholars" can have too specialized a meaning.

Scrolls, the two are not using the same terms of reference; or, to use the colloquial phrase, they are not "speaking the some language." What the scholar means and what the layman supposes him to mean are two different things. And yet, what the scholar knows but fails to communicate to his lay hearer is by no means so recondite or enigmatical that plainer communication would be really difficult.

When theological scholars say, as they have recently been saying, that the discovery of the Scrolls has brought them no information that obliges them to revise their view of Christian beginnings—or at least not extensively—it can be *for them* the truth. But they should go on to tell the laity in what sense it is the truth. What they mean, if they would express it more informatively, is *that they have known for a long time that the traditional view of Christian origins is not supported by history so much as by theology.* Unlike the layman, they are familiar with New Testament historical problems to which it has never been possible to find historical solutions. Dogmatic solutions are another matter. But what the layman thinks he is dealing with in trying to grasp the meaning of the Scrolls is not theology but history, not dogma but fact.

Theological scholars have long been aware, for instance, of the impossibility of knowing, historically, where Jesus was born, or when, or by what means the portrait of him in the first three Gospels (the Synoptics) can be reconciled with the quite different portrait of him in the Gospel of John. This is only the beginning of the matter. Theological scholars know (again as the layman usually does not) something of the extensive debt of Christianity to Pagan religion during the first centuries of its development in the Mediterranean area. Theological scholars have known for some time that there were important resemblances between Essenic organization and that of the early Christian churches and have had reason to suspect that the two may have been organically connected.

The information that comes to them with the discovery of the Scrolls merely adds itself to this earlier information and they say they are not disturbed. Perhaps not. At least, not initially. But should not the layman, who has little if any knowledge of these matters, be given an opportunity to discover whether what is not disturbing to the theologian is disturbing to his own beliefs? Admittedly, the Scrolls, in and of themselves and with no reference to previous knowledge, might not be revolutionary. But the previous knowledge exists. That is to say, it exists for scholars. Why should it not be imparted to laymen also? If the scholar has been able to accommodate himself to historical difficulties by recourse to dogmatic elements, perhaps the layman can do the same. And if not, truth is still a religious obligation. The disputed fourth Gospel scarcely misleads us when it says "the truth shall make you free."

In the sections immediately following, therefore, we shall pursue our investigation by examining some of the information known to scholars. Necessarily, this examination can do no more than disclose the general nature of the situation by exhibiting areas of it that are typical; but this will be enough, no doubt, to remove objections to the introduction of considerations in the later sections, in the light of which the reader can make his own evaluation of the Scrolls.

2. *The Scrolls and the New Testament*

It is a common supposition that we have in the New Testament a self-consistent story of the life of Jesus, followed by a plain account of the beginnings of the church he founded. These assumptions are not true. We do not have the story of Jesus; we have only a fragmentary record. It is not self-consistent; it is contradictory. The account of the beginnings of the church is not simple; it is full of problems. And it is not certain that Jesus founded—or intended to found—the eventual Christian church.

To attest these statements in a way that will allow the reader to verify them without recourse to texts that may be inaccessible or difficult to follow, we shall have recourse to a well-known book, *Peake's Commentary on the Bible,* used freely by the better-educated clergy and available in any good public library. Other commentaries would afford the same testimony, provided they are equal in standards of scholarship. So, of course, would the standard Bible Dictionaries and the reputable textbooks.[2]

First, *that we do not have the story of Jesus but only a fragmentary record:* In the *Commentary's* article on "The Life and Teaching of Jesus," we have the following opening sentences: "The results of critical study of the records concerning Jesus have often been represented as largely negative. The issue is said to be a fresh sense alike of the fragmentary character of our information and of the strangeness of the figure of Jesus Himself. Today we realize that the life of Jesus can never be written. The material is wanting."

Second, *that the record is contradictory:* In the *Commentary's* article on John's Gospel, we read as follows: "The differences between the Fourth and the other Gospels are too obvious to need emphasis. From the second century onwards, they have constituted a difficult problem."

Third, *that the account of the beginnings of the church is not simple but full of problems:* In the article on "The Apostolic Age and the Life of Paul," we are told the following: "It must be admitted at once that our knowledge of the period is disappointingly vague. We begin with a certain number of data with regard to the rise of the Church, data of which the historical value is disputed . . . this lack of definite information is unfortunate, but it is at least a gain to recognize the limitations of our material and avoid the claim to a knowledge which does not exist."

Fourth, *that it is not certain that Jesus founded—or intended to found—the eventual Christian church:* In the article on "Organization, Church Meetings, etc.," we read that "it is a fact of immense importance and significance that Jesus Himself created no organization" but left his movement "pliable, so that it could freely embody itself in any type of organization which varying conditions might suggest." This, however, is a much wider question and scholars cannot ignore the possibility that Jesus expected an immediate Messianic kingdom to follow his crucifixion, in which case there would have been no relevancy in his founding the church that actually developed.

We shall see in the next chapter that the three Synoptic Gospels, although they are broadly similar and based on the same material, also present a problem. What is there, then, that is certain? The historian's answer can only be that nothing is certain. What we have had to go upon is *a consensus arrived at by scholars, a body of informed opinion accepted by seminarians as a standard field of reference or quasi-historical convention which is affirmed by theology as the equivalent of history.*

But it is important that we see the situation as it really is. When new suggestions are made upon the basis of what we find in the Scrolls, they are resisted as though they were gratuitous conjectures, unnecessary and offensive because they fly in the face of findings which have long since been securely arrived at and which should now be left alone. The truth is that the conventional findings have no more been securely arrived at than would have been the case if they had been quite different findings. They are simply the findings that, after surveying the evidence, seemed most persuasive to the minds (or preferences) of scholars.

Let us look at some of this evidence. For the life of Jesus and the story of the early Christian church, we have no testimony from secular history. It is true that there is a brief passage in Josephus, mentioning and praising Jesus, but reputable scholarship has long since rejected it as fraudulent.[3] Our recourse must therefore be to the Gospels themselves in the hope of discovering how much of what is written is a record of events as they actually took place and how much is legendary or theological elaboration.

In this, we have some help at times from the scriptures which were not included in the New Testament, although they were written in the same general period. Let us take an example. It is readily possible for scholars to trace the story of the resurrection of Jesus through its several phases in the New Testament narratives, observing how new assertions were added to meet the objections of unbelievers, and then to extend their investigation to the apocryphal Gospel of Peter, which carries the story to a point which the church fathers, after due trial, found excessive, and so excluded this Gospel from the canon.

Here is the story as given in the Gospel of Peter (circa 150 A.D.):

Now in the night whereon the Lord's day dawned, as the soldiers were keeping guard two by two in every watch, there came a great sound in the heaven, and they saw the heavens opened and two men descend thence, shining with a great light, and drawing near unto the sepulchre. And that stone which had been set on the door rolled away of itself and went back to the side, and the sepulchre was opened and both of the young men entered in. When therefore those soldiers saw that, they waked up the centurion and the elders (for they also were there keeping watch); and while they were yet telling them the things which they had seen, they saw again three men come out of the sepulchre, and two of them sustaining the one, and a cross following after them. And of the two they saw that their heads reached unto heaven, but of him that was led by them that it overpassed the heavens. And they heard a voice out of the heavens saying: Hast thou preached unto them that sleep? And an answer was heard from the cross, saying: Yea (ix, 35-42).[4]

Those who witnessed this remarkable phenomenon, the Gospel of Peter continues, hastened to report it to Pilate, who said that his hands had been washed of the entire matter, and it was thereupon agreed that the witnesses would suppress the report, since, if it became known, it would get them into trouble with the Jews. What we have here is clearly a fabrication, but it merely extends one step further the testimony of the canonical gospels. How then, in this respect, should scholars regard the New Testament record as evidence? Obviously, though written somewhat earlier, it belongs to the same class of literature as the Gospel of Peter.

It is when we go to this larger literature from which the familiar New Testament was selected that we see with fresh vision the kind of testimony that we are dealing with even in the New Testament itself, where doubtless it is at its best. It is not, of course, that the Gospels should be counted unhistorical; the problem is in knowing what is history and what is not. The reader should understand this and thereby see the nature of the evidence upon which the findings of the scholars in the end must rest. He will thus learn how little ground there is for repulsing new suggestions when new evidence is found.

The difficulties encountered in the Resurrection story are matched by the problems presented by the Birth stories. Did the Magi really make this journey or is it based upon the visit of Tiridates of Parthia with the three Magi laden with presents to worship Nero, whom they acclaimed as the Lord God Mithras? Or is it based upon some other story of Magi in search of a Fravashi whose birth had been signaled by a nova in the eastern sky?[5] Probabilities can be weighed and subjective opinions arrived at, but the historical question cannot be solved.

The Annunciation to the Shepherds is in the same category; and the Magnificat and the Benedictus: were they spontaneous song-prophecies, uttered by Mary (some scholars say Elizabeth) and Zacharias, respectively, and recorded by someone who happened to be present, equipped for the purpose? (Luke, chap. i). Or were they liturgical compositions, adapted by Luke to his story? Scholars know that the intrinsic evidence of the passages requires that they be the latter. How much else in the Gospels was drawn from pre-existing sources and likewise adapted to the aims, first of the original composers, then of the editors and compilers? The earliest manuscripts we have, it must be remembered, are no earlier than the fourth Christian century, and by then—indeed, considerably before—there had been time for the church fathers to make many redactions in accordance with the outcome of theological controversy.

It cannot be shown historically that Jesus was born in Bethlehem—or if Bethlehem is accepted as his birthplace, whether it was Bethlehem in Judea or Bethlehem in Galilee. If there was a "Slaughter of the Infants," there is no record of it other than in the Gospels. Herod was quite capable of such a slaughter, but could so barbarous an atrocity have been overlooked by the well-informed Josephus who dwells at length on Herod's crimes? Do we not have here an invention of the writer (or editor) of St. Matthew, who provides the story to fulfill the prophecy of Rachel, weeping for her children? Does he not, for the same purpose of fulfilling prophecies, send Joseph and Mary with the newborn child to Egypt? For the prophecy must be fulfilled: "Out of Egypt did I call my son." So it is with other prophecies.[6]

It is a small matter, relatively, that Matthew gives us the Sermon on the Mount as though uttered all at one time and place, whereas Luke arranges it in sections and connects it with a sequence of incidents. The real question is: How much of the Sermon came from Jesus and how much from other sources?

These examples are but the barest indications of what must be encountered in the quest for historicity in the New Testament scriptures.* But they are sufficient, perhaps, to indicate to the reader the nature and proportionate value of New Testament evidence when it must be considered in combination—or in conflict—with other evidence. It is not that history is absent; the New Testament is quite definitely concerned with historical happenings and with persons active in the development of a religious movement. It is in deciding where the record is and is not dependable that we meet with so much difficulty.

This obviously does mean, however, that when there are new suggestions, such as those arising from the discovery of the Scrolls, it is entirely appropriate to give them full consideration. If they are disturbing to the consensus, or quasi-historical field of reference, formerly arrived at by scholars, it may be because we need a new consensus.

3. Christian Origins and Pagan Influences

The traditional view of the founding of Christianity taken by the typical Christian layman is that Jesus preached its gospel, died as Messiah and Redeemer, arose from the dead and founded the Christian church, which spread out through the world, beginning with the work of the apostles. Or, if he does not believe in the Resurrection, he supposes that the apostles, moved by the spirit of Jesus, founded the church upon his gospel.

He recognizes that Jesus was a Jew and inherited the Judaic tradition. He further recognizes that the apostles drew out the inferences of Jesus' gospel and thus expanded his doctrine; and

---

*The Old Testament presents similar problems but since—to Christians—the question of historicity in the Old Testament has less vital consequences, there is not so much hesitation on the part of scholars in dealing boldly with the outcome of their inquiries.

also that the apostles, because of what they had seen and heard during the lifetime of Jesus and because of their experiences afterwards, came to esteem him as what he had been all along but which they had only partly understood: the Savior and Lord of mankind and Son of God.

In any case, he assumes the originality of Christian doctrine, and it does not occur to him that much of it existed previously (except perhaps as it was foreshadowed by Moses and the prophets), or that a great deal of it is indebted to sources that do not appear in the Bible.

What the layman does not know, and the scholar does, is that there were many Pagan deities during the time of Jesus and afterwards for whom quite similar claims were made and in whose names were preached quite similar doctrines.[7] Mithras was a Redeemer of mankind; so were Tammuz, Adonis and Osiris. The view eventually taken of Jesus as a Redeemer was not a Judaic concept; nor was it held by the first Christians in Palestine. The Messiah the Jews and the Judaic Christians expected was not the Son of God but a messenger from God, not one who saved by blood-atonement but one whose salvation came from his rule of the earth in a Messianic kingdom. The Judaic Christians were not thinking of a salvation that admitted them to heaven, but of a salvation which would establish a new order on earth, and this remained the case, even though they believed in immortality.

It was when Christianity spread out into the Pagan world that the idea of Jesus as a Savior God emerged. This idea was patterned on those already existing, especially upon Mithras. It was the birthday of Mithras, the 25th of December (the winter solstice), that was taken over by the Pagan Christians to be the birthday of Jesus. Even the Sabbath, the Jewish seventh day appointed by God in the Mosaic Law and hallowed by his own resting on this day after the work of Creation, had to be abandoned in favor of the Mithraic first day, the Day of the Conquering Sun.

In the Mediterranean area during the time of Christian expansion, nowhere was there absent the image of the Virgin Mother and her Dying Son. Originally, it was the earth itself that was the goddess, virginal again with every spring. Her son was the fruit of the earth, born only to die, and in dying, to be implanted once more in the earth, as the seed that would renew the cycle. This was the "vegetation myth" from which the drama of the "Savior-God" and the "Mater Dolorosa" was drawn, soon to be elaborated.

The cycle of seasons on the earth was seen to be paralleled by a coordinate cycle in the heavens. There, too, was to be seen the virgin goddess: the constellation Virgo that rose in the eastern sky just when Sirius, the star from the east, was signaling the new birth of the Sun. The passage of the horizon line through Virgo was the conception of the Virgin from the Sun. The earth myth was thus blended with the sky myth and both with the memory of ancient heroes, real or legendary, and so came the saga of the Redeemer.

The cave, later to be associated with the birth of Jesus, was earlier the birthplace of Horus, who, when he was grown, would become Osiris, who must die for the salvation of his people. Isis was the *Mater Dolorosa*. There were innumerable such salvation cults, as described by such writers as Sir James G. Frazer in his *Golden Bough,* and by the great classical scholar, Professor Gilbert Murray.**

In these cults were found the same sacraments later to be called Christian. The Last Supper (Eucharist) belonged to Mithraism, from whence it was borrowed to combine with the sacred meal of Palestinian Christianity. Not only sacraments but such concepts as "the blood of the Lamb" (or of Taurus the Bull) were likewise taken from Mithraism. And not only cultist concepts but ethical teachings too were absorbed from the cults which entered into Christianity. In addition, there were ethical teachings which were not cultist, such as those of the Stoics.

The extent of the indebtedness of Christianity to Pagan religion is so great that, provided there was a Judaic-Christian nucleus at all, very little indeed need have been supplied by the Palestinian Christians. It must be remembered that after the earliest days little was said of Jesus the teacher. It was Christ the Savior who was Lord of the Christians. And whether it had been he or the Lord Mithras would have made very little difference in the redemptionist doctrines, the sacraments and observances of the church that at last declared that "Christ" was the Savior God, a decision formalized by a majority vote in 325 A.D., at the Council of Nicea.

It will be seen, then, that what the scholar knows and the layman does not, is the extent to which Christianity would have become what it did without Jesus and his disciples at all. The only element of importance that is found nowhere in Paganism is the portrait of Jesus the teacher; but this, as we have already noted, was not the emphasis of Pagan Christianity. By the third century, it had passed almost out of sight, not to return until the Enlightenment, the Protestant Reformation, and the invention of printing brought the Bible to the people. The Bible, indeed, had been considered too dangerous a book

* See bibliography, page 132.

to put into the hands of the laity: they were not equipped to understand it and it might be an incitement to heresy. It was the Christ of the Creeds and the Sacraments, the Salvationist God, that the Christian church for so many centuries was concerned with: Jesus of Galilee it scarcely knew at all.

The one essential nexus for making the Judaic Christ the victor in the struggle of salvationist religions was Paul of Tarsus, Pharisee, yet a Hellenist, an inspired Jew with a profound comprehension of Paganism. Supreme master of synthesis, it was he who first conceived the purpose of binding Israel to Athens, the dying Temple of Jerusalem with the Mithraic sacrifice, the Essenic Jehovah with the Unknown God of the Areopagus. As the Apostle Paul, this was the world-minded "Christianos"—never merely a Palestinian Christian—who knew his "Lord" not in the flesh but through his own "gnosis," and saw that Apollos, Mithras and Osiris could be made to bow before his own Hebraic Adonai, and that by absorption of their saviorhoods and blood redemptions, the Messiah of Israel could become the world-Christ.

But it could have happened otherwise and still have borne the name of Christianity. That is what the scholar knows but not the layman. And thus the scholar—not as believer but as scholar—is not disturbed at what the Scrolls imply for Christian origins: he has known all along that *historically,* Christianity is not the religion founded by Jesus and spread abroad by his disciples. But the layman has not known it. The discovery of the Scrolls has somehow made him sense it. That is why his interest in them is not the "fad" that some among the churchmen have tried to make it out to be. The layman wants to know the truth about the origins of Christianity.

4. The Second Battle of the Scrolls: Theology versus History

The first "Battle of the Scrolls" was about their date. There were many who hoped that they did not go back before the beginnings of Christianity. But it is now known that they do: and there is little, apparently, to fan the flames of further controversy.

The second "Battle of the Scrolls" is still being waged. The issue at stake is their significance for Christian origins. It is a controversy hard for laymen to understand. This is because they have not followed—and there is no reason why they should have—the strange trend of modern theology. To the layman, a historical question looks as though it should have a historical answer. If the Scrolls affect our view of how the Christian churches arose, obliging us to recognize that they were evolved from a Jewish sect or sects with many of the same doctrines, similar sacraments and an almost identical organization, then it is necessary to draw some inferences from these facts of history. Christianity, it is evident, was not established through unique events, as the one true church of God, founded by his Son who came to earth to found it; nor are its gospel and its sacraments what we thought they were. Instead of a supernatural intervention, what we have, it seems, is a natural social evolution.

Not so, say the theologians. This matter has been settled, not on historical grounds, which allow of nothing being settled, but by theology. Theodore A. Gill, for example, one of the editors of the independent church weekly, the *Christian Century,* in reviewing Edmund Wilson's book* tells us that "the gravest limitation on Edmund Wilson's report is the era from which it is written. This brand new word about discoveries just now being made is curiously dated in its approach."

Reading these words, the layman cannot be blamed for feeling a little confused. So far as he knows, Mr. Wilson is living in the present age. The magazine for which he writes ("The New Yorker") has no appearance of being retarded by Victorianism. In what sense is he "curiously dated"?

The answer is that he is "pre-neo-orthodox-theological." Mr. Wilson does not realize that the modernist approach to the New Testament scriptures, which sought to understand what they conveyed as history, was interrupted, beginning in the first decade of the present century. It is impossible to settle the problem of the New Testament on the basis of history, the interrupters said. Every question has either so many possible answers that, historically, it is impossible to decide between them, or else it has no answer at all, which is intolerable. The matter must be settled by theology.

Starting with concepts that can be traced back to Saint Augustine and Pelagius (who, as Mr. Gill has perhaps forgotten, are also rather dated in their approach), the theologians worked forward through well-worn paths until they discovered the fecund possibilities of contemporary marriage with the "depth psychology." The offspring is a fascinating progeny of intellectual folklore. It is contended that only through this folklore can mankind be saved. But the reader need not take this any more seriously than the Muslims do, or the Jews,

* *The Scrolls from the Dead Sea,* reviewed, *Christian Century,* October 26, 1955.

who are certain that they will be saved, if at all, without benefit of Christian neo-orthodoxy. This is not to say that one who familiarizes himself with the concepts of the neo-orthodox theology will not learn to understand its ancient vocabulary in a more modern and viable way than he might at the beginning expect, but the effort is not necessary. The laity on the whole have quietly understood this and have respectfully left the new theology alone.

But what is its relation to Christian history? In a brilliantly perceptive article which takes up this very question, Duncan Howlett, an independent-minded theologian,[9] shows how "the modernist movement," which "represented the coming to full flower in Protestantism of the fact-minded point of view, the conviction that faith ought not to be based upon theology," is now reasserting itself through the laity. He quotes one of the theologians who says that the interest of the public in the Scrolls is "morbid." Mr. Howlett does not think so. "The desire to know what the Scrolls contain and what these writings mean," he says, "rises from a deep-seated yearning on the part of people everywhere to learn more about the enigmatic figure known to men as Jesus Christ." People are not satisfied, he concludes, "with a Christ of faith." They "also want to know everything [that can be known] about the Jesus of history."

What the theologians have done, if we survey it realistically, is similar to what is known as "circular reasoning." They have set up theology to be the judge of history; and yet, being Protestants and unable to separate their theology from the Bible—the Bible, indeed, being its necessary foundation—they have relied upon this very Bible, the historical problems of which they could not solve, to support a theology based upon these unsolved problems. This theology in turn undertook to solve the historical problems which, in their unsolved form, had been adopted as its basis!

We are not here concerned, let it be noted, with any other aspect of the new theology than its relationship to Christian history. With this, however, we are very much concerned. For what we have is an empty pretension. What they were unable to do as historians, theologians have undertaken to do as theologians. But as theologians they have nothing to stand upon except the Christian history which was an insoluble problem to them. What they thought they could do was to rely upon faith to determine fact. But how was faith to be determined? If the New Testament narrative was not factual, how could one have faith in its principal figure? How could one know, apart from knowledge of fact, that one's faith was not divorced from reality?

In answer to this it was urged that most history is in doubt. Nothing can be known to have occurred as it is said to have occurred, and even if we know the form of an event, do we know its meaning? So faith is necessary in any case, before history can be seen to have specific meaning. As an ultimate kind of skepticism, the argument is certainly tenable. But it is not a position which can be a sound foundation for Bible-based theology. The truth or falsity of the main events recorded in the New Testament and the implications of those events—also as recorded in the New Testament—must be determined *historically* before there can be enough reality for Bible-based theology to rest upon. In other words, you cannot make Christian origins something that they may not have been merely by believing what you wish about them. You can make an imaginary world that way, in which to live and think and—through its symbols—worship, but you are out of touch with the real world. So the case for theology as arbiter of history falls down.

Mr. Wilson, of course, did not know that it was ever supposed to have stood up. So he becomes "curiously dated" in his approach. Mr. Gill says that the uniqueness of Christ has never been located in his teaching; it is "the uniqueness of the One whom faith has discerned in him . . . the uniqueness of what believers claim happened in him and happens in him and nowhere else." But the layman, still possessed of a sense of history and eager to remain in touch with reality, feels rather uncertain that by believing the theology of the present he can determine the events of the past.

The second "Battle of the Scrolls" may therefore be one that the theologians cannot win. It may even be a rather decisive battle for the entire question of theology versus history. The thing about the Scrolls that makes them so formidable is their tangibility. They *exist*. Can theology, through faith, make them disappear? The *implications* of the Scrolls are also quite substantial. Can theology make shadows of them? Here we have not only the manuscripts themselves, but the caves, the monastery ruins, the baptistries, the scriptorium—and thereby history comes to life. In the presence of the Scrolls as fact, other facts become discernible. The Scrolls not only exist for what they mean in themselves: they become signposts, direction-markers on the chart of history. The Essenic sect of Qumrân, through its Scrolls, "being dead, yet speaketh." And what it speaks of points to new answers to old questions, answers which can grow to be very large and give a new and more natural account of Christian history.

5. The Early Church and the Essenic Sects

"If there are but superficial parallels between the Essene Teacher of Righteousness and Jesus of Nazareth," writes Professor Frank M. Cross, Jr., one of the scholars working on the Scrolls, "there are intimate parallels between the Essene and primitive Christian communities."[10]

The most immediately evident of the parallels is in the organization of the two societies. When the entire community met as a congregation, in each case it was called "the Many." From "the Many" were chosen "the Twelve," to represent the twelve tribes of Israel. Jesus tells the twelve "disciples" whom he appointed to be his inner circle that they were to be enthroned as judges over "the twelve tribes of Israel." In the early church, "the Twelve" are likewise important, and there, as in the Qumrân sect and among the Essenes generally, we find an "Inspector-Superintendent" or overseer, such as was James the Just who presided over the church at Jerusalem.

Both communities have "all things in common." Wealth must be contributed to a general treasury, in the care of a steward; so also with wages currently earned. The steward disburses from the common treasury whatever monies must be paid out for the community's expenses. Here there irresistibly comes to mind the story of Jesus and the man who had "great possessions." "Go, sell all that thou hast," commands Jesus, "and give to the poor." Since "the Poor" was one of those terms used by the Essenic sects to indicate their own societies, Jesus was in effect telling the wealthy man to join such a sect, meeting its requirement that he contribute his riches to the common fund. Since Jesus adds to this command an invitation to "come, follow me," the interesting question arises as to whether in joining a sect of "the Poor," in which he could at the same time follow Jesus, the wealthy man would not have been joining a sect to which Jesus himself already belonged.

Both in the Qumrân community and in the Christian churches, there were rules providing penalties for fraud in connection with the common fund. The Christian rules seem to have been much stricter. In the Manual of Discipline, one who "commits a fraud against the wealth of the community, causing it loss, shall repay it in full. If he is not able to pay it, he shall be punished sixty days" (1QS, vii, 7–8). How he is to repay the loss if he has given all he possessed to the community, it is difficult to see. Perhaps the meaning is that if he still has the sum that he withheld or stole, he must surrender it, or otherwise suffer two months of deprivation. The Christian* rule was more severe. In the book of Acts (v, 1-11), we read that Ananias "sold a possession and kept back part of the price," his wife, Sapphira, being "privy to it." Peter, having discovered the fraud, tells Ananias that he could have done whatever he liked with the money while he regarded it as his own, but that having offered it to the common treasury with the pretense of complying with the rule, he had not "lied unto men, but unto God." Whereupon the terrified Ananias immediately expired, followed a few hours later by his wife, Sapphira, who in equal terror "gave up the ghost" when she heard herself condemned. Whatever else we may deduce from this dramatic story, we can scarcely suppose that the penalty for fraud against the common treasury was less than excommunication.

Peter, in this narrative, unquestionably looks upon the contribution of wealth to the common fund as voluntary (until the purpose of contributing has been declared)—or perhaps only a part of the individual's possessions were required for contribution. But elsewhere we are told that "all that believed had all things in common, and they sold their possessions and goods, and parted to all, according as any man had need" (Acts ii, 44-45). And again "the multitude of them that believed were of one heart and soul: and not one of them said that aught of the things which he possessed was his own, but they had all things in common" (Acts iv, 32). It is apparent that the Essenic and Christian practices regarding the communal treasury were quite similar, and the spirit reflected in the writings of both groups when the common fund is mentioned is the same. The common treasury was a practice expressing brotherliness, unity, oneness of heart; for the entire life was to be communal: in peace and harmony the "believers" were to walk with one another, each seeking, not his own advantage, but the advantage of all.

Both groups also had a rule requiring that if an accusation were made against a brother, it must first be made privately, then in the presence of three (sometimes two) witnesses. If the accusation still stood and no agreement had been reached as to what should be done about it, the disputing parties and the witnesses must go before the congregation of "the Many," where the matter would be finally set-

---

* We are using the word "Christian" in this section (as sometimes elsewhere) in the generally canonical sense as a matter of temporary convenience. Whether the group discussed was at this time "Christian" in the sense traditionally assumed is a semantic and historical question to be taken up later (Section 9).

tled. Only "the Many" had the power of excommunication.
This rule, sometimes called the *correptio fraterna,* is peculiar
(so far as is known) to the Essenic sects and the Christians.

Baptism was practiced by both groups, and although it is
not known that Christians ever practiced daily baptism as
the Qumrân community did, neither is it known that the
Essenic sects in other places followed precisely the ritual of
Qumrân. Differences in subordinate provisions of the ritual
do not affect, however, the underlying basis of the practice,
which was "repentance unto remission of sins" and the re-
solve "to fulfill all righteousness." The same basic significance is found also in the baptism of John. In all these cases,
the baptized were admitted into a community that expected
the coming of a Messiah.

Here, too, the Essenic sects and the Christians had a
basis in common. The "Anointed" whose appearing they
awaited was one with whom they were already "in communion" through a sacrament. The Christians expected the
"Anointed One" to be Jesus; but it is not certain that the
Messiah of the Essenes was the Teacher of Righteousness.
In the case of the Christians, unlike that of the Dead Sea
monastics, it was one Messiah they looked for, whereas the
Scrolls speak of two. It is quite possible, however, that eventually the two became merged into one in the Qumrân anticipation, and it is altogether likely that many varieties of
Messianic expectation were eventually harmonized by the
Christians in the process of conversion and absorption
through which they prevailed.

The Essenic sects and the Christians were alike in being
the peoples of a "New Covenant," a term which has the same
meaning as "New Testament." In the case of the Judaic
Christians this was a Sinaitic covenant, a return to the law
of Moses, as it was with the Qumrân sect and the Essenes.
It was Paul who dispensed with the Mosaic requirements, to
facilitate the progress of the Gentile church.

The sacred meal of the Qumrân sectarians was closely similar to the early Christian sacrament of the Lord's Supper. An
element in the Qumrân ritual that seems at first divergent and
rather curious is the "presence" of the "Anointed Ones" of
Aaron and of Israel, with no plain indication as to whether
they were regarded as physically present or participating in
the meal in some mystical way. But since we must suppose
that the monastics were currently using this ritual rather than
waiting for the coming of the Messiahs before they could
use it, it is natural to accept the mystical interpretation.

Professor Cross, who definitely sees the symbolic presence

of the "Anointed Ones" as "the liturgical anticipation of the messianic banquet" finds the resemblance of this feature of the sacrament to "the later eucharistic practice of the Palestinian church . . . very strong."[1] In the account of the Last Supper as observed by Jesus we are told (Mark's Gospel) that he used the words, "Truly I say unto you, I shall not drink again of the fruit of the vine until that day when I drink it new in the Kingdom of God" (xiv, 25). Jesus is thus identifying himself with the Messiah anticipated in the sacred meal of the Essenes (and of his own community?) and informing his hearers that he will not again participate in the sacred meal *as a communicant* but only when he has become manifest as the visibly present Messiah. In the Pauline account of the Christian Last Supper, there is again this clear connection between the meal and the Messiah represented in it by anticipation. "As often as you eat this bread and drink the cup, you proclaim the Lord's death until he comes" (I Cor. xii, 26). Here, however, is the commemoration of the death of the Messiah as well as the anticipation of his reappearance.

In the Qumrân liturgy, it is provided that "the Messiah of Israel shall stretch forth his hands on the bread; and after giving [asking?]* a blessing, all the congregation of the community shall partake, each according to his rank" (1QS, later fragment). It was essentially this ritual that Jesus followed, as related in the New Testament accounts of the Last Supper. "And as they were eating, he took bread, and when he had blessed, he brake it and gave to them" (Mark xiv, 22). It will be noted that the meal was already in progress and that the sacrament was observed in the course of it, reminding us of the description of the actual meal (not "token") that was eaten at Qumrân, too, where also the liturgical observance must have been interpolated.

The further words of Jesus, identifying the bread with his body and the wine with his blood, may well be a further duplication of the Essenic liturgy of which we do not have the written version. In the physical absence of the Messiahs, they must in some way have been represented. Possibly they were represented by priests or by other appointed celebrants; this is likely since a hand had to be "stretched out" to ask the blessing, following which the bread had to be broken. But it may have been felt that no individual could symbolically represent a sacred mystical presence, so the bread itself must represent it. In ancient times, sacredness was attached not

* There are breaks in the manuscript fragment requiring that the most likely words be supplied as indicated by the context.

only to bread, but to all food, especially to food a portion of which had been offered to a god (thus the "blessing"). But bread was the staple article of diet, more freely available than other foods, and symbolically it stood for food of every kind. For this reason (though by no means for this alone) it was a sacred element in the sacraments of mystery cults in many places.

It seems altogether likely, therefore, that the bread represented the Messiahs of Aaron and of Israel in the sacramental meal of the Qumrân covenanters, and of the Messiah, perhaps differently envisaged, in the Essenic sects more generally. What Jesus did (and in doing it, occasioned no surprise, apparently, in the minds of those present) was to identify *himself* with the bread that had long represented the Messiah in sacred meals with which his disciples were already familiar. Instead of saying, "This bread is [represents] the Messiah of Israel," he said, "This is [represents] *my* body," thereby claiming to be himself the Messiah.

Or, alternatively, the person representing the Messiah at the Essenic sacred meals may have spoken *in his name;* in this case, he may have said (speaking for the Messiah), "This is my body," and thus the words the disciples heard from Jesus may have been the exact ritual words to which, as members of an Essenic order, they were accustomed.

The case of the wine would be similar, wine also (the "blood" of the grape) being sacred. The ancients knew nothing of the chemistry of fermentation (not only as to wine but also in the "miracle" of the yeast leavening bread). Consequently, they regarded the effect of wine as "god-possession." The god had entered into and "enthused" them (the literal meaning of the word *enthused* means possessed by a god) and so they were filled with fervor (or frenzy). The earlier orgies associated with the magical properties of wine slowly gave way to more restrained and solemn observances in which "possession" *by* the god changed into communion *with* the god and the magical became the mystical. Thus, in the mystery cults of the Mediterranean area, the wine that was "blessed" was the blood—and therefore the life—of the Redeemer. For our covenanters at Qumrân, it was the blood—the life—of the Messiahs. Through the bread that was flesh and the wine that was blood the Messiahs were present with their people. Through the bread that was broken and eaten, and the cup that was passed from one to another, the Messiahs entered into the very life itself of their communicants and all were as one, mystically united.

This, then, was the Essenic sacred meal, so close as to be

almost identical with the sacred meal of the early Christians. That the two were organically related, it is scarcely reasonable to question. The early Christian sacrament *was* the Essenic sacrament with, *perhaps,* some Christian adaptations. We stress the *perhaps* because there is no certainty that the accounts of the Lord's Supper in the New Testament have not been edited to accord with the practice (and doctrine) of a later time. As we have seen earlier, it is difficult to know when the New Testament is giving us actual history and when it is giving us history that doctrine has elaborated. But at the very least, Dr. Cross is right in seeing that the parallel between the Essenic sacred meal and that of the Palestinian Christians was "very strong." Since the Essenes were predecessors as well as contemporaries of the Palestinian Christians, it is immediately evident which group derived its sacred meal from the other. There is only one alternative possibility: if the Christians did not derive their sacred meal from the Essenes, then the Christians were themselves a sect of the Essenes. To this, however, we shall come in a following section.

Further similarities between the Essenic sects and the early Christians are evident in their common view of world events, which they believed were hastening towards a cataclysmic consummation, after which would come the realm of God, inaugurated by the "Anointed One" (or "Ones") of Jehovah. The people of "God's lot" were in a terminal struggle with "the sons of Belial"; the "Sons of Light" were fighting the ultimate battle with the "Sons of Darkness." Essenes and Christians alike were at the center of a cosmic conflict which had reached its ultimate phase and would soon be brought to a decision.

The parallels between Essenic scriptures—the Scrolls and the other literature which, because of the discovery of the Scrolls, it has been necessary to redate—and the Christian scriptures are so marked and so numerous that it is necessary to conclude that they belong to the same system of Messianic doctrine, the same sectarian religious movement, the same development within Judaism which, in the one case, remained Judaically Essene and Christian, and in the other, expanded into Gentile Christianity.

Concerning these parallels between Essenic and Christian scriptures, Dupont-Sommer points out that in Brownlee's annotated translation of the Manual of Discipline, there are so many references to "parallel texts in the New Testament" that it gives the translation an "austere and despoiled appearance," which nevertheless is "the most eloquent of

proofs."[12] Professor Cross, an admirable though perhaps
somewhat less adventurous scholar, gives the following similar opinion: "In these new texts we are in the conceptual
world of the New Testament. The New Testament and Essene
writers draw on common resources of language, common
theological themes and concepts, and share common religious
institutions. They breathe the same atmosphere, confront the
same problems."[13]

And thus it must be acknowledged that between the Essenes and the Judaic Christians there was the closest of relationships: this at the very least. The question still to be
answered is whether this was all. Was it relationship or was
it identity? Did the Christians borrow or were they a sect of
the Essenes?

6. More About Scriptures Not in the Bible

We have indicated that one of the effects of the Qumrân discoveries has been the need to redate documents which were
formerly thought to belong in the Christian era. Wherever
fragments of a manuscript have been found in a cave the
documentary contents of which have been dated as to the
time of their deposit, we know that the manuscript is at least
as old as the time when it was placed in the cave. Through
internal evidence that relates it to other documents—or
which in some other way determines its chronological context in the light of the new discovery—we can arrive at the
approximate period during which it was written. This has
meant, as we have already observed, that documents that
were thought to be of Christian authorship have been found
to be in fact Jewish.

We shall now more specifically describe such documents
and interpret the consequences of their redating. A book
which has long been known to scholars and which has presented unusually perplexing problems bears the title *Testaments of the Twelve Patriarchs*. It is one of the scriptures
used by early Christians but which it was decided to leave
out of the Bible. Its form will seem rather strange to modern
readers since it employs the device of presenting what it has
to say as though it were an anthology of final utterances of
the twelve sons of Jacob, or Israel. This sort of device—
writing in the name of heroic personages of a former time
—was not uncommon in the centuries immediately before and
after the beginning of the Christian era.

The *Testaments* are transparently a production of this general period—but of which century? Scholars formerly thought that the *Testaments* were Jewish in their original form but with extensive Christian interpolations and editing.[14] On this basis, however, parts of the document were utterly baffling. R. H. Charles, the greatest of all scholars in this field, called one chapter (Levi xvii) "unintelligible."[15] Indeed it was, considered as a Christian writing.

There was no solution until fragments of the book were found in the caves. Its date being thus fixed, and its literary context much better known, we may now reconsider it and revise the former view of Christian interpolations. This has some rather important consequences. For one thing, we must acknowledge that when the document refers to Christ it does not mean Jesus. As we have pointed out in a previous chapter,* the word that in English we pronounce *Christ* is a translation of the Greek word *Christos,* which in turn translates the Hebrew word that we call *Messiah*. As we have previously emphasized, the word is not the name of a person but the title of an office. A Messiah or "Anointed One" could be any of a number of persons, in the past or the present or the future. A Hebrew king was an "Anointed One"; his enthronement was accompanied by an anointing with oil which had the significance of making him Jehovah's elect, a sacred person. David, we remember, was unwilling to slay Saul, although he had been grievously provoked and Saul was hunting him down to take his life. David's reason was that he could not face the guilt of having shed the blood of "Jehovah's Anointed."

In the first century B.C., however, the "Anointed One" had come to mean what we have understood it as meaning in previous sections: the agent of God who would appear at the "ending of days" to judge the world and establish a new order. But this was not any one person to the exclusion of other possible persons. We are re-emphasizing this matter, even though we have pointed it out before, so that the reader will see clearly that in the first centuries B.C. and A.D. Jesus was by no means the only person who could be meant by *Christ*. The scholars who worked on the *Testaments of the Twelve Patriarchs* before the discovery of the Scrolls did, however, suppose that Christ must mean Jesus, and thus they were misled. One of the reasons why they thought Jesus must be the only possible person who could be meant was the "Christian" quality of the teaching that the book contained. They did not think it possible that teaching of this sort could emanate from any group earlier than the first century Christians.

* Chapter 3, Section 9.

We must now see that the *Christos* of the *Testaments*, who could not have been Jesus, may very well have been the Teacher of Righteousness. But whether he was or not, the contents of the document, although owing nothing to Christianity, was used as a Christian source book. The *Testaments* and the letters of the Apostle Paul have so many points in common that Canon Charles, without benefit of the recently available information, remarked forty years ago that "St. Paul seems to have used the book as a *vade mecum*."[16]

Not only the letters of St. Paul, however, but the Gospels themselves have been influenced by the *Testaments of the Twelve Patriarchs*. The following is an illustration. "I was sold into slavery and the Lord of all made me free; I was taken into captivity, and his strong hand succored me. I was beset with hunger, and the Lord Himself nourished me. I was alone and God comforted me: I was sick and the Lord visited me; I was in prison, and my Lord showed favor to me; in bonds and he released me." That is from the *Testaments of the Twelve Patriarchs* (Joseph i, 5–6). Now this: "For I was hungry and ye gave me meat, I was thirsty and ye gave me drink, I was a stranger and ye took me in, naked and ye clothed me, I was sick and ye visited me, I was in prison and ye came unto me." That is St. Matthew's Gospel (xxv, 35).

In the same way the *Testaments* anticipated some verses in the Sermon on the Mount. There are differences in every case, but they are obviously differences by adaptation, differences by amendment. The dependency of the one document upon the other is too plain to admit of doubt. Again, let us turn to Canon Charles: "The Sermon on the Mount," he says, "reflects in several instances the spirit and even reproduces the very phrases of the *Testaments of the Twelve Patriarchs*."[17]

Since the *Testaments* go further than the Scrolls towards what has been thought of as the specifically Christian ethical outlook, it has to be considered that Jewish teaching, at least in some of the sects, developed to a point where it approached and paralleled the later Christian teaching—and to an extent that made it an important resource for Christian writers, such as those who composed the Gospels (in their original form), and the Apostle Paul. It is true that we knew already of such noble-minded teachers as the Pharisee, Rabbi Hillel. But what we know now directly connects Jewish and Christian teaching in a way that raises the question as to whether in this respect Christianity was merely indebted to Judaism or was not, in fact, an organic part of it until the Gentile church was founded.

At the very least, as Professor Dupont-Sommer has put it, "The Christian tree only grew so far and so vigorously because the soil in which it germinated had been so marvellously worked."[18] But this is indeed the least. For it seems more and more possible that at the beginning, Essenic Judaism and Palestinian Christianity were one and the same plant.

Let us turn, however, to another non-Biblical document, of equal importance with the *Testaments* for the understanding of early Christianity. This is the *Didaché*, or *Teaching of the Twelve Apostles*.[19] Here, as in the Dead Sea Scrolls, we have the Two Ways, "the Way of Darkness" and "the Way of Light." The Greek version of the *Didaché* contains references that are clearly Christian. But a Latin version is known that omits many of these references. The document from which the Latin version was translated therefore did not have them either. The Greek one must have been a Christian revision. When scholars studied the Latin version, they concluded that it could not be a Jewish source since it had no Jewish prototype. Otherwise, they would have called it Jewish. Now, of course, there *is* a Jewish prototype. The *Didaché* belongs with the same literature as the Dead Sea Scrolls, but appears to have been edited by early Christians. And it contains not only language and ideas familiar to us in the Christian scriptures but also baptism after fasting, and a rather curious version of the sacramental meal. The sacred wine, the *Didaché* tells us, represents "the Holy Vine of [God's] son, David." The bread symbolizes the "life and knowledge [made known] through Jesus, [God's] child." Do we have here a possible link between Jesus and the Essenes? The wine represents the Jewish King David, and the bread the Jewish prophet, Jesus, who was called the Son of David. Can this be the way in which the Essenic sacrament, at least in some of the sects, made room for Jesus? It will be noted that instead of the Messiahs of Aaron and Israel we now have David and the Davidic Messiah. Was this a variant preferred by some of the sects that did not seek a priestly Messiah but only a Messiah of Israel? Surely, what the new knowledge is revealing to us is the natural, historical evolution of Christianity from a branch of Judaism which preceded it.

In another non-Biblical but important document, *The Shepherd of Hermas*,[20] which formerly was regarded as Christian but with inexplicable features, such as the fact that Jesus is nowhere mentioned although there is a lot of what seems to be Christian theology, we have a further document from Essenic sources. The Catholic Church at one time regarded this book as canonical, then later changed its mind: so close is it to Christian teaching. But we see now that Jesus is not mentioned in it because its author did not know of Jesus, or, if he did, did not regard him as the Messiah or the Son of God

that he speaks of. Once more, the question may be raised:
Is the reference to the Essenic Teacher of Righteousness?

We cannot at present answer these questions that point to
the Teacher of Righteousness. Perhaps we shall never be able
to answer them. But we can certainly answer the question as
to whether Essenic and Palestinian Christian religion belong
together. Here in the *Shepherd* is a book that the Catholic
Church was so sure was Christian that for a time it was included in the canon. It reflected, so it seemed, Christian
theology. But it was Judaic, one of the books of the movement
that produced both the New Covenanters called Essenes and
the similar New Covenanters who came to be known as Christians. Once again, we ask, was the relationship closer than this?
Were there two merely similar groups, or, until the coming of
Gentile Christianity, were they one and the same? Was there
any more difference between the first Christians and the
Essenes than is conveyed by the exchangeable terms, the "New
Testament" and the "New Covenant"? We shall ask this question more precisely later on.

7. *Hypothesis and Conjecture*

The information conveyed by the foregoing sections may have
suggested to the reader how great the need has now become
for a review of what we have called the *consensus** arrived at
by scholars concerning the New Testament. In this section we
shall take up one particular instance in which a new suggestion
should be considered, namely, the Gospel of John.

We have mentioned at various times the problem that
scholars must face in trying to reconcile this Gospel with the
other three. Let us take up a little more precisely what the
problem is. The first three, or Synoptic,** Gospels tell much
the same story. There are discrepancies, but it is possible, to a
considerable extent, to reconcile them. John's Gospel, however,
tells quite a different story from the other three. If John is
right, then the other three are wrong; if the Synoptics are
right, John's Gospel must surely be in error. First, in the case

---

* For the definition of scholars consensus, see page 86.
** Synoptic. From the Greek, συνοπτικοῦ, *taking a common view;*
from συν, *together;* ὀπτι, *see; seen together.* The first three, or
Synoptic, Gospels are considered to be based in large part on an
earlier version of Mark's Gospel, *Ur-Markus,* and a document
known as *Q,* from *Quelle,* the German for *source.* They treat the
material thus derived in quite different ways, but it is identifiably
the same material, and the events recorded are viewed from the
same general standpoint.

of John, the subject matter is different. Jesus is quite another sort of teacher. Second, the public life of Jesus is much longer. Instead of a few months or a year we have nearly three years. Third, the locality in which Jesus does his work is different. It is Judea, chiefly, instead of Galilee. Fourth, Jesus is the Messiah from the beginning of his ministry and walks almost majestically through a divinely appointed program. In John's Gospel, too, we have, for example, the story of the raising of Lazarus from the dead, of which there is no mention in the other Gospels. Yet this was an event—if it happened, or even appeared to happen—which would have been difficult to overlook. The fact is, as scholars of all persuasions have felt bound to attest, that in John's Gospel we have a new and different view of Jesus which the Synoptic Gospels do not support.[21]

If dogmatic elements are introduced, it is possible, of course, after a fashion, to bring the two portraits together. You can believe what you want to believe. But as a matter of historical scholarship they cannot be brought together. The Scrolls, however, one of which contains a verse which John's Gospel almost paraphrases,* offer us a suggestion. Heretofore, scholars had supposed that John's Gospel could only have been written rather late—say between 90 and 110 A.D.—and by someone who lived, to quote one of the scholars, "where Jewish and Hellenic thought met." But we now know that John's Gospel could have been written much earlier, and in Palestine. Jewish and Hellenic thought had met and mingled in the Essenic sect that produced the Scrolls. Zoroastrian thought had also had its influence, and there is no difficulty whatever in supposing that John's Gospel was composed by an Essene or similar sectarian. But if so, where did he get all this discourse which is attributed to Jesus? We do not know but we can offer a suggestion. This sort of discourse—

> I am the Way, the Truth and the Life; no one cometh unto the Father but by me. . . . Peace I leave with you; my peace I give unto you. . . . Not as the world giveth give I unto you; let not your heart be troubled, neither let it be afraid. . . .

This sort of discourse, sonorous and liturgical in tone and entirely different from the language of Jesus in the first three

---

* The verse is John i, 3: "All things were made by him; and without him was not anything made that hath been made." Here is the Manual of Discipline parallel: "Everything that is he establishes by his purpose, and without him it is not done." (It must be remembered that John's Gospel is in Greek, the Manual in Hebrew. The slight difference in the phrasing of the verse in the two documents could be largely accounted for by the Scroll writer having "thought" in Hebrew, the Gospel writer in Greek.)

Gospels, would be quite appropriate to the Essenic Teacher of Righteousness, the exalted priest and prophet who suffered martyrdom and may have been expected to reappear as the Messiah, and the writer of John's Gospel may have combined some of the Teacher's doctrine with a reconstructed life of Jesus.

On this subject, Millar Burrows remarks that "more than in any other part of the New Testament, contacts with the Dead Sea Scrolls have been noted by many scholars in the Gospel of John. . . . The whole manner of thinking and the literary style [of John] are strikingly like what we find in the Qumrân texts . . . priestly and liturgical—as though, it has been said, the Gospel was written to be read aloud in a cathedral."[22]

Or again, in the words of Professor K. G. Kuhn, of the University of Göttingen, "The parallels with the teaching of Jesus and the Synoptic tradition are numerous and significant. But the profound relationship with the Gospel of St. John seems to be even more important. . . . We succeed in reaching in these new texts the 'mother-nurture' of the Gospel of St. John."[23]

We are not, in all this, advancing a definite thesis, but we can venture the suggestion that it opens the way to a more probable explanation of John's Gospel than any that we have had in the past. Certainly, it is incumbent upon scholars to pursue this line of inquiry to the full extent of the knowledge that becomes available, irrespective of its effect upon previous views of the unsolved problem of this fourth Gospel. It may be objected that in the past we could at least relate John's Gospel entirely to Jesus. The answer is that this could be done dogmatically but not historically. To the extent that we adhered to the Synoptics, to that extent were we unable to believe John. The further answer is that we should seek the truth without regard to what it will turn out to be.

If John's Gospel is an Essenic theological treatise in the form of a biography of Jesus, and if it incorporates some of the doctrines taught by the Teacher of Righteousness who preceded Jesus, it is of greater interest for those reasons, not less. In the past, we have not known where to look for the sources of John's thinking. There have been guesses, but none of them were very productive. If it now turns out that the sources for John's Gospel may well be Essenic liturgics and theology, the quest for better understanding of it should turn in that direction.

It is true that this is following a conjecture. But that is what historical scholarship is supposed to do—follow a conjecture until it can be seen whether or not it makes a working hypothesis, and, if it does, follow the hypothesis until it is proven wrong or right. All that we have now is conjecture— a *consensus* of conjecture. When it was first suggested that the Synoptic Gospels were based upon two sources, Mark (later Ur-Markus) and "Q," this was conjecture, but it has worked out as a viable hypothesis and much better than those that preceded it. It is the same thing that should be done with John's Gospel—indeed with the entire literature of the New Testament—in the light of the knowledge that comes with the Scrolls.

Meanwhile, let us note once more—even though we are dealing only with hypothesis—how we keep coming to the same position: that the Christian church, in its organization, its sacraments, its teaching and its literature is related—and in its early stages may have been identical—with the New Covenanters who were known as Essenes, some of whom wrote the Dead Sea Scrolls.

8. Some Questions That Invite New Answers

One of the consequences of the new knowledge which has come into our possession with the Qumrân discoveries—and which is still accumulating—is the way in which it revises our understanding of events and circumstances in the New Testament narrative. Although as yet more questions are raised than answered, they are questions that in themselves imply a changed viewpoint. What in the past was so often silhouetted against a blank background is suddenly seen in its natural context. Although this does not mean that we are immediately able to establish a firm relationship between an event or discourse and this new context, it does mean that in many cases we can see indications clear enough to suggest that they be explored.

In taking up some of these indications in this and the following section, we ask the reader to remember what was said at the beginning of the chapter: that we are not protagonists of particular hypotheses or anxious that suggested explanations be sustained; we are eager only that there be an honest effort—diligent and responsible but not held back by an excessive reverence for tradition—to give to what is told us in the canonical scriptures its most natural and probable interpretation. What follows merely illustrates what the approach of such an effort might be.

What are we to say, for instance, in the light of our new knowledge, of John the Baptist who the Gospels tell us was

brought up in the desert, the wilderness of Judea? Can we any
longer imagine him wandering about, sustaining himself somehow in solitude in the unrelieved desolation of this wilderness
and then coming forth and preaching a doctrine that is only
coincidentally similar to that of the covenanters whose monastery was in the area where John is reported to have lived?
Where did John get his ideas? And his ascetic practices? And
his baptism? It is true that he departed from the ideas of the
Dead Sea sect, but it is also true that he had to have some ideas
from which to make departures.

Where else shall we look when the evidence points so plausi-
bly to the Qumrân monastery? That John was, in the broader
sense of the term, an Essene can scarcely be doubted. In this
same broader sense, were not his followers also to be numbered with the Essenes?

Jesus was baptized by John the Baptist. Some of his disciples were drawn from John's following. Can Jesus, any more
than John, be thought of as having been unconnected with
Essenic communities before he decided that John's version of
the Messianic faith was the one he was ready to adopt? Just
as Jesus later made considerable departures from John's emphasis, had not John previously made similar departures from
the emphasis of the community to which he had belonged?
We say "had belonged," but actually we are not entitled to
assume that John had left this community or had been expelled
from it because of nonconforming practices any more than
we need assume that in establishing his own teaching, Jesus
had made a definite break with John.

How did Jesus find his disciples? Why were they twelve in
number? Were they—or some of them—his brothers in one of
the Essenic sects? How better can we account for their lack
of hesitation in laying aside the matters in which they had
been employed and immediately joining him? Surely, in the
mission to which he felt he had been called, he needed to set
up at least a simple organization, and so he used the pattern
of the Essenic sects and called to himself from his own sectarian community these men whom he knew and made them
his Twelve. Whether he himself forsook this community—and
if so, when?—is a question to which we will come a little
further on.

There is a story in the Gospels which tells of Jesus disputing
with scholars in the Temple when he was only twelve years
old. Some commentators have thought this story more likely
to be legendary than the report of an actual event. But suppose that Jesus was taken when he was a boy—as we know
other boys were—to be taught by "the masters" in one of the
Essenic sects? Not only would he learn the "canonical" scrip-

tures—those that all Jews accepted—but also the sectarian
writings with their special point of view. What difficulty is
there, then, in seeing Jesus as an unusually responsive student
who already had committed many of the scriptures to memory
and who, being Essenic, was contending in the Temple against
the Pharisaic scholars, who were fascinated by his use of
proof-texts, and glad to keep him talking so that they could
marvel at so much learning in one so young?

It may seem as though we are assuming too much in supposing that Jesus was brought up as an Essene. But he was
certainly not brought up as a Sadducee; and in view of his
hostility to the Pharisees, he is not likely to have been brought
up in that sect either. So it was an Essenic sect or nothing.
As Jesus obviously knew the scriptures well, it is impossible
that he had not been schooled. We cannot believe, then, that
he belonged to no sect at all. Thus, even by a process of elimination, we see the strong probability that his education was
Essenic, and as we know from previous sections, his teaching
and his entire outlook relate him to the Essenes.

In sending out his disciples on a missionary campaign, Jesus
tells them that they shall go forth "by two and two," taking
"a staff only, no bread, no wallet, no money in their purse"
(Mark vi, 7–8). How were they to be maintained? Where would
they sleep? Who would feed them? In the past, the only answer
that could be given to these questions was that there were hos-
pitable people in Galilee who would do these things for strangers with a religious message, or else that the disciples of Jesus
were unusually well equipped with relations and friends. What
now immediately leaps to mind is the suggestion that they were
expecting to be received in the Essenic colonies which we
know existed in the cities and villages, as described by Philo
and Josephus. From the Damascus Document, too, we learn
of "the session of the cities" and that there were "camps."
Since the disciples of Jesus belonged to the Essenic movement,
they were entitled to hospitality in accordance with its rules.

But Jesus anticipates the possibility that they will not in-
variably be welcome. Not all of the colonies or camps are
favorable to Jesus, perhaps because of his claim to be a
prophet. (We are leaving out of account the contested question as to whether Jesus, at this point—or at any—made a
larger claim than this.) In the event that the disciples were not
received by the colonies, they had instructions from Jesus as
to what to do. "And whatsoever place shall not receive you,
and they hear you not, as ye go forth thence shake off the
dust that is under your feet for a testimony unto them"
(Mark vi, 11). Which in itself has an Essenic flavor!

Where did Jesus spend his "forty days in the wilderness?"

Perhaps the phrase is metaphorical. Some commentators have thought so, believing that a literal sojourn of several weeks in a deserted place was unlikely. Perhaps they are right. But we see now how they may have been only partly right. Jesus would not have had to spend these several weeks unsheltered. He could have gone to the monastery at Qumrân. He could have lived for a while, as some of the monastics did, in one of the caves. After fasting, he might have noticed some of the stones that are so abundant in this area, and wished that they might be "turned into bread." Indeed, it could have been more than a wish: hunger brings on precisely such hallucinations. And he saw it as a temptation to believe in magic, in his power to perform a miracle, and quoted a verse from the scriptures he knew so well: "Man shall not live by bread alone."

A much more controversial hypothesis may be suggested as a new and more illuminating interpretation of the expulsion of Jesus from "Nazareth" after he had identified himself as the one predicted by a passage in the book of Isaiah. (We will leave to the next section the question of whether Nazareth was an actual city or a much wider area. Luke's Gospel merely says that Jesus "came to Nazareth where he had been brought up: and he entered, as his custom was, into the synagogue on the sabbath day.")

It has usually been assumed that in the cities of Palestine at this period there was a synagogue in each city, of which all the inhabitants who wished to do so made use, both for sabbath worship and for instruction in religion. This may indeed have been the case. But we do not know. The origin of the synagogue is shrouded in obscurity. Even the name itself involves questions that it would take many pages barely to outline. In Greek—and the word *synagogue* is Greek, not Hebrew or Aramaic—the primary meaning is *an assembly* rather than a building. There is, of course, a Hebrew word that the Greek word translates. But this, too, means an assembly, originally for any purpose, but eventually almost always for religious purposes.

The question that arises, however, in the context of this story in Luke's Gospel (iv, 16–30) is whether the "general" synagogue, if such existed, was not a meeting place of the Pharisees. It was they who developed the synagogue as the word is usually construed. Did Essenes attend the Pharisaic synagogue? Or did they make their own quite independent provisions? Everything we know from the Scrolls indicates the latter. So does what we know about the Essenic sects from our other sources. If Essenes and Pharisees observed the sab-

bath together, in a common place of worship, the fact is so
remarkable that it would revise considerably our view of the
relationships between the Jewish sects.

Where, then, did Jesus go when he went to the synagogue?
Was it to the synagogue of the Pharisees? It seems hardly
likely. He was sharply opposed to the Pharisees and criticized
them freely. In the light of our new knowledge, linking him
so definitely to the Essenic sects, it is all but certain that he
went to the meeting place of an Essenic order—indeed the
very community where, to use Luke's language, "he was
brought up." In this case, the "synagogue" was not a building,
so designated, but an assembly, a sabbath meeting of "the
Many." May we not suppose, then, that he belonged still to
this community, and having become widely known as a
teacher, it was appropriate that "the Many" should desire to
hear him and consequently had a scroll of Isaiah delivered to
him, so that he could read and expound it?

The passage Jesus chose was from the sixty-first chapter
(1 and 2). "The Spirit of the Lord is upon me, Because he
has anointed me to preach good tidings to the poor: He hath
sent me to proclaim release to the captives, And recovering
of sight to the blind, To set at liberty them that are bruised,
To proclaim the acceptable year of the Lord." This prophecy,
said Jesus, when he had given back the scroll to the attendant,
was there and then being fulfilled. And the assembly marveled
at the excellence of his exposition. Presently, however, having
warned them that he did not expect them to believe him,
since a prophet is never "acceptable in his own country," he
told them that he himself was the "Anointed" who was fulfilling the Isaiah prophecy.

To the assembled "Many," this was blasphemy and they
hastened to "cast him forth," even trying to throw him down
headlong from a precipitous place at the brow of a hill, but
he managed to escape them. Was this the rejection of Jesus
by his own sect? Is it an indication of what he meant when
he warned his disciples that some of the Essenic "colonies"
might not receive them? And what he had in mind when he
lamented that there were places where he could do nothing
"because of unbelief"?

As we shall see later, no matter what the case was with the
Essenic and early Christian communities, Jesus, as the Gospels
depict him, besides giving evidence of belonging to an Essenic
order, also shows many signs of independence—and even of
being critical of certain Essenic practices.

None of the above is set forth as assured exegesis. All that
is intended is the application of our new insights to events

that may become more meaningful if we can learn to see them in a clearer context. Any one hypothesis may be set up only to be knocked down by further information or clearer perception; but it then becomes possible to erect a better hypothesis, and this is what scholars should be doing.

One of the most perplexing of New Testament problems is the question of how it came to be that the Jerusalem church was ruled by James the Just. What happened to the original Twelve *as such* we do not know, although we know something of the activities of a few of them such as Peter. Peter himself, however, although an influential figure among the Jerusalem Apostles, was less so than James the Just. The latter seems to have had his own Twelve and to have arrived at the superintendency of the Jerusalem church with no association with Jesus during the time of his ministry. He is said to have been the brother of Jesus ("brother of our Lord"), but this has led to many difficulties such as the doctrinal one of maintaining "the perpetual virginity" of Mary and the historical one of explaining how James acquired a position which Jesus in the Gospels seemed to have given to Peter.

Moreover, we learn from the Church Father Eusebius, quoting Hegesippus (circa 160 A.D.), that James was "holy from his mother's womb, drank no wine nor strong drink, nor ate animal food: no razor came on his head, nor did he anoint himself with oil nor use the bath. To him only was it permitted to enter the Holy of Holies. . . . His knees became hard like a camel's, because he was always kneeling in the Temple, asking forgiveness for the people."[24]

The description here is that of a Nazarite. Why did Mary dedicate James "from his mother's womb" to Nazaritic austerities and do less than that for Jesus? Let us, since we cannot answer the question, accept the assertion. But there is a much harder question: How could James enter the Holy of Holies which the High Priest himself was only permitted to enter once a year? Moreover, what does it mean that he kneels in the Temple, constantly asking forgiveness for "the people." Was it because he saw in James too dangerous a rival that the High Priest Ananas had him assassinated, for which he was deposed by Agrippa II? That the community over which James presided did spend a good deal of time in and about the Temple is attested, apparently, by the story of Paul and the riot that occurred there, incited by the charge that Paul was no longer a faithful Jew.

Eusebius also quotes a lost book of Clement of Alexandria, *The Institutions,* in which Clement writes that "Peter and James and John, after the ascension of our Saviour, though they had been preferred by the Lord, did not contend for the honour, but chose James the Just as bishop of Jerusalem."[25] From this it would seem that the three who had been closest to Jesus felt unequal to the situation that confronted them after his death—or that they came to feel so after a time— and nominated James to be the superintendent of the community in which they were the most natural leaders.

But what *was* the community over which James presided? His prestige was evidently very great, and with a large number of people. The title "the Just," "the Righteous," is definitely of the Essenic variety, and even reminds us of the Teacher of Righteousness. If the chronology allowed it, James would have to be seriously considered as the one to whom this name was given. But he would need to have lived at the very least half a century earlier. Even so, he was plainly a man of wide influence among the Jews of the period. It is also clear that he was definitely Judaic. He made certain concessions to Paul so far as the Gentile churches were concerned, but his own community was of Moses' law, Essenically organized, and looking for a Messiah.

The fuller analysis of the problem of James, bishop of Jerusalem, would carry us farther afield than is appropriate to the scope of the present work. It is much to be wished that there are scholars with the intrepidity to conduct such an analysis in the light of our new knowledge with an objective attitude towards the outcome. But it is in any case clear that the figure of James casts a very wide shadow. Now that we know the Essenic sects and the Christian apostolic community were so extremely close in organization, in sacraments, in doctrine, in the Messianic hope, must we not ask whether James the Just was the leader of the entire movement? And must we not suppose that the group that had been led by Peter accepted its position as subordinate to James because he was the revered "high priest" of all the Messianic Jews, the acknowledged head of all the sects that belonged to the New Covenant?

This leads us, however, to questions that we shall take up in the next section.

9. *Who Were the Early Christians? Some Suggestions for Further Inquiry*

In our discussion of Christian origins down to now, we have taken what might be called a generally canonical position.

That is, we have assumed for the most part the centrality of
the New Testament tradition even while we have been reviewing and evaluating it.* If we had not done this, there would
have been no meaningful way of unfolding to the reader the
significance of the Scrolls in their effect upon the standard view
of early Christian history. It may not have escaped notice,
however, that, so far as we could do so without hindrance to
communication, we have avoided the use of such names as
"the Christian church," "the Essenes," "the Essenic sect" (sin-
gular), in a way that would indicate that we were speaking
of separate bodies. To have assumed that Christians and Essenes were independent entities, closely related but external to
each other, would have put too great a strain upon the evidence.

What we had in mind was the question that we now must
raise. How certain is it that the position that we have called
"generally canonical" is unassailable? The Scrolls, in what
they imply about Jewish sectarianism in the first century A.D.,
invite us to inquire *without preconceptions* just when it was
that what we now call Christianity actually became such. This
is obviously too large a question for a detailed treatment in
our present survey. But the question itself, and how it arises,
we have some obligation to explain.

Let us again notice that those to whom the name *Essene* is
given did not use that name in speaking of themselves. Nor
was the name *Christian* used by those who are called the early
Christians. The people who came to bear these names called
themselves "the saints," "the brethren," "the elect," "they
that believe," "they that are in Messiah [Christos]," "they that
are of the Lord," "the Sons of Light," "the disciples," "the
Poor," "they that are of the Way," and other similar appel-
lations.

Only three times in the entire New Testament do we find
the word *Christian*. The first is in the book of Acts (xi, 26),
where we are informed that "the disciples" were called Christians "first in Antioch." This means that they were given
the Greek name for "Messianists," something that had not
previously occurred. Mostly, they would still be known as
Jews. But within the Judaic grouping, their distinctive doctrine
made them "Christianoi."**

* See footnote, page 74.
** We will use this term in this section to keep the reader reminded that we are not speaking of Christians as they were later
identified. We will also use "Essæi" rather than "Essenes" (following Philo, who emphasizes the widespread nature of the movement).

The second mention of Christianoi in the New Testament is also in the book of Acts (xxvi, 28). King Herod Agrippa says to Paul, "Almost thou persuadest me to be a Christianos." Agrippa probably meant it in derision. He was himself a king in Israel, an "Anointed One," and therefore quite literally a "Christos" of the existing order. Sarcastically, he speaks of adopting the superstition of an eschatological "Anointed One," the King of Israel who will found a new order.

The third mention is in the first of the letters attributed to Peter (iv, 16). "But [if a man suffer] as a Christianos, let him not be ashamed; but let him glorify God in this name." The implication here is that the disciples regarded "this name" as opprobrious. The writer of Peter says, "Accept it and turn it into praise to God."

Since in cases two and three—the third being unmistakable—the name Christianoi is a term of derision, so probably was it in the first at Antioch. It should be clear then, that the first century "followers of the Way" did not refer to themselves as Christianoi.

In the case of the Essæi, the name does not appear in the documents recently found nor in any of the books that might be called Essæic. The names that appear in their writings as those they applied to themselves are the same as those used by the Christianoi.

For the latter, however, another name was used in the New Testament and appears twice. We read in Matthew (ii, 23) that Jesus is to be called a "Nazarene." In the book of Acts (xxiv, 5) Paul is referred to as "a pestilent fellow, and a mover of insurrections among all the Jews throughout the world, and a ring-leader of the sect of the Nazarenes." We also know from some of the early Church Fathers that the Christianoi were originally called (and apparently acceptably) "Nazarenes," a name that is supposed to be derived from the name of the city from which Jesus came: Nazareth.

But scholars have always had to accept the possibility that *at the time of Jesus* there was no city called Nazareth. They have resisted this possibility, it is true, and sometimes quite vigorously, but it definitely remains, as the reader may discover for himself by reference to the standard Bible dictionaries.[20]

Moreover, Nazareth is not mentioned either in the Old Testament or the Talmud. This is an argument from silence but is not negligible. Of far greater weight, however, is the silence of Josephus. For besides being a widely traveled writer who never missed anything and who described voluminously all that he saw, *Josephus was the Jewish commander-in-chief in*

the war with the Romans in Galilee, which war he describes at
great length and yet never mentions Nazareth. This, too, is
said to be an argument from silence, but it might be observed
that it is a very profound silence. If Nazareth was an important Galilean city, as so many of the scholars insist, how did
Josephus fight a war in which all the resources of Galilee were
mustered and overlook Nazareth?

The scholars allow, however, that there is a strong possibility that Nazareth, instead of being the name of a city, is a
synonym for all Galilee. In this case, "Nazarenes" would mean
the same as "Galileans," and we know that the Christianoi
were called Galileans as late as the time of the Emperor Julian.
What this amounts to is that the Essæi of Galilee were sometimes called Galileans, sometimes Nazarenes, and that they
became strongly identified with a Galilean—and therefore a
Nazarene—whose name was Jesus.

There is still a further possibility. Matthew, who was always much concerned for the literal fulfillment of prophecy,
tells us that Jesus went to Nazareth (Galilee?) so that "it
might be fulfilled which was spoken by the prophets, that he
should be called a Nazarene." The only prophecy known to
us to which this could refer is the one in Isaiah (xi, 1) that
there shall be a "shoot" or offspring of Jesse "and the spirit
of Jehovah shall rest upon him, the spirit of wisdom and
understanding": one of the passages connected with the
Messiah. Since the word for "shoot" (netzer) * is the root word
for Nazarene, it is considered that the Nazarenes may have
been a Messianic sect, perhaps connected at some time with
the Nazarites, a sect of ancient origin (it will be remembered
that James the Just followed Nazaritic practices), whose emphasis was the Messiah of David, Jesse's son. If so, what we
have is another Essæic sect, and one that existed before the
time of Jesus.

So again we find the distinctions fading. "Nazarene" means
"believer in a Messiah." So does "Christianos." And we
know that all the Essæic sects believed in a Messiah. The
truth about Nazareth may well have been that it was a Nazarene encampment or monastery to which Jesus and James both
went, either as blood brothers or as brothers in the community. Some scholars find in the word Nazareth the meaning
of a "watchtower," and this, too, is quite plausible since there
was a tower connected with the monastery at Qumrân. There
is nothing the people of this period and area liked better than
to find a word with many meanings so that it had cryptic as
well as self-evident significance.

* Hebrew: נֵצֶר.

If this be the true construction of the matter, we can understand the rise of James to pre-eminence as that of an inspired ascetic whose piety and benevolence made him widely revered and brought him at last to the leadership of all the New Covenanters, Galilean, Judean, and perhaps even Samaritan, who would presently be numbered with the Christianoi. Meanwhile, Jesus, who had not been vowed to asceticism, lived a freer life and finally became the Prophet of the Nazarenes, and, after his martyrdom, was gradually accepted by the entire movement of New Covenanters, with the exception of such communities as resisted this consolidation—perhaps such as the monastery at Qumrân. But as to that, we do not know what happened after the monastery was destroyed— only that manuscripts of the later "Christian" literature were deposited in caves somewhat farther away in the second century A.D.

And now, we must broaden the canvas a little before we conclude. It has long been evident to scholars who were willing to interpret the testimony in its most natural way that what are known to Christian history as "heretical" Christian sects were in fact movements which began before the first century A.D. Gnosticism is one such sect. "The Gnostics," says Professor Gilbert Murray, foremost scholar in this field, "are still commonly thought of as a body of Christian heretics. In reality there were Gnostic sects scattered over the Hellenistic world before Christianity as well as after. They must have been established in Antioch and probably in Tarsus well before the days of Paul or Apollos. Their Saviour, like the Jewish Messiah, was established in men's minds before the Saviour of the Christians." And Professor W. Bousset, whom Murray quotes, gives us his verdict: "If we look close, the result emerges with great clearness, that the figure of the Redeemer as such did not wait for Christianity to force its way into the religion of Gnosis, but was already present there under various forms." [27]

To open up this field further would take us to the Church Fathers, particularly the heresy-hunter Epiphanius, who, in his extreme zeal, is often careless and lets us see what the true conditions were. We would need to consider the Nazoreans, the Iessaeans, the Therapeutae (claimed to be originally Christian although they were known to Philo as having been long in existence before 25 A.D.!). This is a field too much neglected by scholars. Some of them should break out of the "canonical consensus" and search the patristic literature in the light of the new discoveries and of what we have come to learn about the Essæic and Gnostic movements and their counterparts throughout the Mediterranean world.

When this search is made, what is suggested here will become completely evident: that in what is known as the beginning of the Christian era, there existed not only in Judea and its adjacent territory but throughout the Mediterranean area a considerable number of religious movements of which the Essæi, the Gnostics and the Christianoi were typical, and that in the first three centuries—particularly the second and third—there was an intense theological struggle within and between these movements. Not until this struggle was decided —in the third century—did there emerge what we now know as Christianity.

The reader will now, it is hoped, have sufficient understanding of the historical questions which the discovery of the Scrolls impels us to review to see with some clearness that those scholars are right who are saying that the study of Christian origins must be drastically revised. Can there be any doubt, when the discovery is seen in its appropriate perspective, that the finding of the Scrolls is "revolutionary"? Can it possibly be maintained that our "understanding of the New Testament" is not "substantially affected"?*

Christianity, we must now see, instead of being a faith "once for all delivered to the saints" in the Judea of the first century, is a development of one branch of Judaism into a religion which presently, when it mingled with other religions in the Gentile world, developed by a natural evolution into the religious system, widely divergent within itself, that we know today. The other main branch of Judaism, the Pharisaic, followed the rabbinic tradition, exalted the Torah, and was also affected, although in a less degree, by the Gentile world until it evolved into the Judaism we now know, with its three classifications of orthodox, conservative and reformed.

In the light of new knowledge, do these two religions seem diminished? Shrunken by truth? Safe only if they rest on fable? Moses and the Galilean—do we hear them less plainly if God speaks to us through them in a more natural way? Surely, there is a sounder basis for religion. "He hath showed thee, O man, what is good; and what doth the Lord require of thee, but to do justly, to love mercy, and to walk humbly with thy God?"

* See page 85.

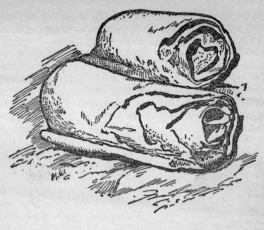

5

The Scrolls and Jesus

1. Schweitzer's View of Jesus

One of the things that is most feared—and it must be admitted that there are grounds for it—is that the new knowledge flowing from the discovery of the Scrolls will affect our portrait of Jesus. We say "portrait" because, as we have seen earlier, a true biography of Jesus cannot be written. The material available is too uncertain and, in any case, is insufficient. But on certain terms, it is possible to arrive at what we have called a portrait.

What scholars have hoped for, if they have been traditionalist in faith, is that the Gospels, in spite of the problems they present, would permit a portrait of Jesus as a universal Savior and Lord. On the other hand, if their faith has been more modernist or liberal, they have hoped that Jesus could be portrayed as a prophet and teacher with a contemporary and timeless significance.[1]

To arrive at the first kind of portrait is extremely difficult—even impossible—without recourse to theology. The questions to be answered are, of course, *not* theological but textual and historical. If, however, we choose to introduce a theological criterion when we treat these questions, we can get the portrait that we want—but it will be theological.

To arrive at the second kind of portrait was once regarded as much easier. Liberal scholars such as Renan appeared to have made considerable progress, but this was interrupted near the beginning of the present century. The result of this interruption has not been to restore the traditional portrait but to make more difficult than ever the discovery in the New Testament narrative of any kind of portrait that is self-consistent and meaningful to modern minds.

The scholar who more than all others produced this hiatus was Albert Schweitzer. In his monumental work, *Von Reimarus zu Wrede,* published in German in 1906 and translated into English in 1910 with the title, *The Quest of the Historical Jesus,*[2] he advanced the thesis that Jesus was, in Jesus' own view, the Jewish Messiah who brought death upon himself in the expectation that it would result in a *parousia** or manifestation of himself as the "Anointed One" of Israel. Schweitzer's thesis was formidably supported by his rigorous appeal to the actual testimony of the Synoptic Gospels. He insisted upon remaining with these documents, including all the eschatological portions of them, which the liberal scholars had decided were insertions made by the writers of the Gospels—or by revisers of the original writings—to make the Gospels accord with prevailing eschatological ideas.

The liberal scholars, thought Schweitzer, had been just as bad as the traditionalist ones in allowing subjective considerations to influence their work. There was no more reason for discrediting the eschatological sections in the Gospels, or the Messianic consciousness which the Gospels attributed to Jesus, than for discrediting any other section. The liberals, swayed by their own view of what most naturally should have occurred, could not believe that Jesus had accepted the Messianic doctrines in the form in which he found them, or that he had identified himself with the Messiahship of Israel so literally. It was not concordant with the remainder of his teaching. The Gospel writers were not likely to have been able to invent or insert from other sources the parables and the discourses which seemed to have nothing to do with a Messianic role; so they must have inserted the eschatological passages so as to make Jesus fit what had come to be the prevailing view in the apostolic period when the Messianic expectation had become dominant.

* Greek: παρουσία, *a becoming present, an arrival.* Used especially of the anticipated hour in which the Messiah would be seen to be such.

What, for example, was to be made of such a passage as the following?

> But immediately after the tribulation of those days, the sun shall be darkened and the moon shall not give her light, and the stars shall fall from heaven, and the powers of the heavens shall be shaken: and then shall appear the sign of the Son of man in heaven: and then shall all the tribes of the earth mourn, and they shall see the Son of man coming on the clouds of heaven with power and great glory. And he shall send forth his angels with a great sound of a trumpet, and they shall gather together his elect from the four winds, from one end of heaven to the other (Matt. xxiv, 29-31).[3]

How was this to be reconciled with the doctrine implied in "the Kingdom of God is within you," and the metaphor of the yeast slowly leavening the world until it became at last the abode of peace and good will, of love and brotherhood, which Jesus seemed to have promised? How could Jesus have preached both cataclysm and gradual progress both at the same time? The liberal scholars, not quite unreasonably, decided that the Jesus of the "inner Kingdom of God" and the realistic slow advance of man towards perfection was the one his chroniclers could scarcely have invented, whereas nothing was more likely or more natural than that the Gospel writers should have derived the Messianic passages from the apocalyptic literature familiar to them and have adapted these passages to the story of Jesus.

Schweitzer said that on the contrary there was no reason whatever for supposing this except that it suited the outlook of the liberal scholars.[4] Jesus had lived in a former time. He could have had a quite different view. The only sound thing to do was to take the scriptures as they stood and see what inferences could be drawn from them. Holding strictly to this position, at any rate as to the eschatological references, Schweitzer developed his own interpretation. No traditionalist himself, he nevertheless would yield nothing to liberalism or to anything whatever at the expense of close adherence to the New Testament record. The result was an exposition diametrically opposed to the liberal viewpoint: Jesus did indeed regard himself as Israel's Messiah.

Schweitzer may still be wrong. Liberal scholars as well as more traditional exponents would be happier if he could be proved so.[5] The present writer does not hide for a moment his own wish that the liberal view might be restored. But wishes and expectations are two different things; and always it is truth that should prevail. And so we say again, the liberal view is *possible*: the portrait of Jesus as non-Messianic teacher may still be right; the eschatological elements in the Gospels may indeed be insertions. But it seems less likely than it used to seem. And this is because of the effect, more indirect than direct, of the Dead Sea Scrolls.

What is it that has happened to make Schweitzer more likely to be right? So far as was known when Schweitzer wrote, the eschatological movement in the time of Jesus did not have much of the particular content that Jesus seemed to supply. According to Schweitzer:

> The Baptist and Jesus are not . . . borne upon the current of a general eschatological movement. . . . There is silence all around. The Baptist appears and cries: "Repent, for the Kingdom of Heaven is at hand." Soon after that comes Jesus, and in the knowledge that he is the Son of Man lays hold of the wheel of the world to set it moving on that last revolution which is to bring all ordinary history to a close. It refuses to turn, and he throws himself upon it. Then it does turn and crushes him. Instead of bringing in the eschatological conditions, he has destroyed them.[6]

Schweitzer—quite excusably—was wrong about there being no general eschatological movement which provided the context for John the Baptist and for Jesus. We now know that there was. The idea, moreover, which became especially persuasive to Jesus—that the Messiah must be "a suffering servant of God" who might have to die to bring about the new world order—was already considerably developed when Jesus gave his attention to it. Professors Brownlee and Dupont-Sommer have shown that there is a considerable probability that this view of Messiahship was already far developed at Qumrân, and Dupont-Sommer has even associated it with the Teacher of Righteousness.

Let us go then with Schweitzer to the record as we have it, and see how the Messiahship of Jesus is depicted in the New Testament.

2. Jesus as Messiah of Israel

Nowhere in the Synoptic Gospels, even accepting the record exactly as it is, do we find a clear indication that Jesus regarded himself as the Messiah from the beginning of his ministry. But it cannot be said to have been impossible. In any case, as Schweitzer points out, a time came when Jesus sent out his disciples to proclaim the coming of the Israelic Kingdom of God, and he told these disciples that before their mission was completed the Kingdom of God would already have appeared. His command to them, according to the

Gospel, was: "Go not into any way of the Gentiles, and enter not into any city of the Samaritans, but go rather to the lost sheep of the House of Israel." In other words, he was the Israelic Messiah and expected his *parousia* within a few weeks. But it did not happen. And when it did not happen, there came a change upon Jesus, so that, as the record describes it, he was "transfigured." He began now to talk of going to Jerusalem and of undergoing suffering and death. According to Schweitzer, this is because he had adopted—perhaps he had tended towards it all along—the view already mentioned that the Messiah must be "the suffering servant of God" who was prophesied (Isaiah, liii), and so only through his agony could he force the appearing of the divine kingdom.[7]

From the new documents and from the effect they have upon our understanding of the material we already possessed, both Biblical and non-Biblical, this begins to seem a probable interpretation. It was Jesus alone, says Schweitzer, who in the first place thought of himself as the Messiah. Others had thought of him only as the prophet who would precede the Messiah. We know now much better than we did before that this expectation of a preceding prophet was characteristic of New Covenant Messianism and current at the time. Messianic believers such as those of the Qumrân community expected that the Messiah of Aaron, who would be a priest, and the Messiah of Israel, who would be a descendant of King David, would be heralded by a prophet, and the latter role was the one that Jesus—so his followers thought—was then fulfilling. In the Gospels, this forerunner was to be a reincarnation of Elijah.[8]

John the Baptist, from his prison cell, sent messengers to Jesus to ask whether he, Jesus, was this prophet. Jesus answered in very guarded language. Indeed, it was scarcely an answer at all. Later, Jesus explained to a few of his disciples (the "Three") that it was John the Baptist himself who was Elijah, the preceding prophet, and that he, Jesus, was the Messiah. He asked them to keep it secret. But Peter, in a moment of enthusiasm, blurted it out and all twelve came to know of it. This, says Schweitzer, was the secret which Judas betrayed to the Jerusalem priests and which gave them a perfect pretext for doing away with Jesus.

It certainly was an ample basis for the charge of treason. Not only could blasphemy be charged on Judaic grounds, but the Roman authorities, with little belief in "kingdoms not of this world," would recognize in an "Anointed One" a pretender to the Jewish throne, an insurrectionist who wanted to be king. Of these they had already seen enough; no province was so hard to keep in order as Judea. So the priests could depend on the Romans for complete cooperation.

But what of Judas? Why did he inform the authorities? Certainly not for "thirty pieces of silver." It must have been that he, bolder than the others, saw himself as acting out a part that was essential to Jesus' plans. For on the basis of Jesus' own disclosure, he sought death, expecting that it would bring on his *parousia:* his manifestation as Messiah. And so, when Judas later hanged himself, it may not have been in remorse so much as in desolate disillusionment. The *parousia* had not happened; Jesus was not the Messiah.

Irrespective, however, of the role of Judas, Jesus brought death upon himself deliberately, says Schweitzer; and in the light of the new knowledge it looks rather more possible that he did. We shall also have to admit that the death of Jesus did not bring on the Messianic kingdom. Perhaps we must listen anew to the tragic words spoken from the cross, "My God, my God, why hast thou forsaken me?"[9]

Yet, according to the New Testament narrative, the Nazarenes who had been his followers did not concede that Jesus had been mistaken. They felt that he was still alive: that his manifestation would come later, within their own generation. Their community slowly took form within a larger community; other New Covenanters joined them in their hope. And thus there came to be established what, canonically, is known as the Judaic Christian church.

What happened to this church? At first, it was the focus of the new movement, through being centered in Jerusalem. The disciples of Jesus belonged to it, and some of them were prominent in it. But when the war came that ended in the fall of Jerusalem, in 70 A.D., this church migrated to Pella in Transjordan. That ended its prestige. Probably it survived as an unimportant segment of the later Ebionites.[10] As the Messiah of Israel, Jesus must therefore be said to have failed. His special expectation found no fulfillment, whether miraculous or a natural historical one.

Meanwhile, through the activity of the Apostle Paul, a Gentile church grew up which Jesus had in no way anticipated. Instead of Jerusalem being the center, it was Rome. Instead of the "lost sheep of the House of Israel" being rescued, redemption was proclaimed in the name of Jesus to the entire Mediterranean world. Gradually, as we have seen, this Gentile church became part of a development that finally resulted in a Christianity which, instead of being the hope of a Messianic kingdom, was a syncretic system formed from many religions and destined to be expressed in varying ways through many sects and many churches.

3. Jesus as Timeless Teacher

Where, then, does this leave Jesus? It leaves him, says Schweitzer, as a man who belonged to his own time, whose thinking was quite different from ours, who believed himself to be a Messiah in a way which for us can have no meaning. Jesus cannot be turned into a teacher who crowned his life-mission with martyrdom. He was, from first to last, imbued with the Messianic expectation of his age and regarded himself as chosen to fulfill it.

This may be. And yet a weighty question still remains. We think of the man who told the parables. The impression that he leaves is vivid. The Parable of the Good Samaritan, the Parable of the Prodigal Son: there is an ethical sweep here that owes nothing (or need owe nothing) to a Messianic expectation. Moreover, there are contrasts—sharp ones—between Jesus, as the Gospels tell us of him, and anything we know as yet about the Jewish sects. The Essenes were very particular about orders of precedence. Everyone was junior to somebody and must take orders from his senior. But Jesus had no use for this: he said that the greatest is the servant of all and not above menial tasks; and to dramatize it he washed his disciples' feet. It seems as though indirectly he is rebuking the Essenic sects.

The people of the sects were ascetics. They ate only the meals prepared by the community. Jesus was not an ascetic. He accepted hospitality freely. He complained that he was being called a wine-bibber. He was also described as the friend of publicans and sinners, namely, of tax gatherers and their women. And when he was asked to give an account of this, he said, whimsically but pointedly, that those who are whole need no physician, so he spent his time with the sick. If Jesus was once a monastic, he was certainly not so as depicted in the Gospels. Nor does he seem to be dependent for his teaching upon a group of which he was a member. "He taught them," St. Matthew's Gospel says, "as one having his own authority and not as their scribes." These features of the life of Jesus are just as significant as any others, and they point to an independent and impressive figure, a powerful personality.

We must reckon also with the extent to which Jesus felt himself able to supersede the Mosaic law. It is true that he said he came "not to destroy but to fulfill" the Torah. But even the necessity he felt for making such an explanation illustrates the distance he had traveled. He revised the *lex talionis;* instead of "an eye for an eye, a tooth for a tooth," he commanded that men should "love their enemies." Possibly, there were

127

others among the New Covenanters who had gone this far.
Some of the teachings in the Jewish scriptures which the Scrolls
have redated—the scriptures not in the Bible—approach this
ethical level. Yet, there is a certain boldness to the teaching
of Jesus. One senses a personality, an independent mind, an
intense spirit.

It is noteworthy that Jesus was not strict about keeping the
sabbath—although the sectarians decidedly were. "The sabbath," he said, "is made for man and not man for the sabbath."
This does not sound at all like the Israelic Messiah of the
eschatological passages. We are not here in the atmosphere of
the Qumrân monastics. Or of anything that is even touched
with asceticism. Can it be that Jesus broke rather sharply with
the sect of which he was a member? Did he attract his following because his religion was brighter: "My yoke is easy," he
said, "and my burden light." And did the "Galileans," the
Nazarenes of his sect who had gathered about him, afterwards
retreat from this? Did they forget? We do not know.

There is still the teaching of the "Kingdom of Heaven within you," and it is hard to reconcile with the expectation of a
cataclysm. The life of Palestine was full of stress. The people
wanted to throw off the rule of Rome and put an end to the
corruption of their own leaders. Especially, they hated the
Romans. But, said Jesus, "If a member of the Roman garrison
compels you to act as his porter for one mile, go with him
two miles. If the contemptuous invader strikes you on one
cheek, turn the other."

Or again, "Return good for evil; love your enemies. God
sends his rain on the evil and on the good alike; be equally
impartial. Be perfect as your heavenly Father is perfect." This
is in a different mood entirely from the brooding Messianic
foreboding, to be followed by a supernatural glorification.

Religion can be summed up, said Jesus, in two principles:
"Love God sincerely and other people as much as you love
yourself." As for ethical problems with which so many were
then engrossed, studying them so pedantically, the matter
can be put into a single sentence. Jesus said: "Do unto others
as you wish them to do unto you." He did not invent these
summaries of "the Law and the Prophets," but he makes his
emphasis clear by the fact of selecting them.

Or again, "Do not make long prayers," he says, "asking
God for foolish things. He knows what is good for you better
than you do, and needs no prompting to keep him interested.
When you pray, try to understand what God wants from you;
it is much more important than what you want from God."

"Spend no more time than is necessary, worrying about
material things. Anxiety of this sort, besides being useless and

unnecessary, spoils the joy you ought to take in living. Observe other forms of nature—the birds and flowers: they don't worry about the cost of finery; yet even the regal Solomon was not better arrayed. Get your mind on what is really vital: the Kingdom of God and how you can serve it; then everything else will take its proper place and you will not be disturbed by a bad sense of proportion."

"When you are busy telling other people what is wrong with them, pause occasionally and take a look at yourself. You can see better where the splinter is in your brother's eye if you take the block of wood out of your own. Beware of false claims, especially by people who profess to be religious. False prophets can be known to be such by watching their behavior. 'By their fruits ye shall know them.' It is not correct belief, the conforming creed that will save you; nor yet by saying, 'Lord, Lord,' to me. It is the kind of life you live that defines you; and that is the way I shall identify my followers."

And much else in the same vein. We have translated freely and colloquially, moving somewhat into a modern vocabulary. The Greek of the Synoptics is equally colloquial: so presumably was the Aramaic that was used by Jesus, so that he spoke plainly and easily, in a language the people could understand.[11]

Jesus was not always somber. He could be humorous and whimsical. If some one tried to trick him in an argument— which happened rather often at first—he adopted a humble pose and deftly led him on until he was caught in his own trap. It is reasonable to believe that Jesus enjoyed this—and at the same time was compassionate. He was not always tranquil. Sometimes his invective was rather terrible. As has often been noted, he was particularly harsh on the Pharisees.

His method of teaching was most engaging, perhaps, when he invented fables—or parables, as we call them—to drive home a point. "Put new wine into old wine-skins," he said, "and you lose both, the wine-skins by breakage and the wine by spillage." So it often is with old institutions and new teachings. Such illustrations produced immediate comprehension. On the other hand, parables like that of the Sower were not obvious in their meaning, but when requested, Jesus would explain such parables. The Parable of the Good Samaritan is known universally, and teaches that our neighbor is anyone who needs our help. The Parable of the Prodigal Son teaches that forgiveness is not dependent upon sacrifices or atonements but is a free gift of God, who recognizes repentance a long way off and goes half way to meet it. On the basis of this parable, not only does the need for Redeemership disappear, but even the Messianic apocalypse seems unreal and far away.

We have given this summary of the teaching of Jesus—or a part of it—so that the reader may see why the liberal scholar finds it hard to believe that such a Teacher sought death as the Israelic Messiah. But life and history are all the things they are: not some of them. And so the mystery of Jesus remains.

4. *The Word Still Spoken*

Meanwhile, many people will feel deprived because of the new knowledge since it seems to take away much that has been thought dependable—a process, however, that has been going on in any case, ever since the beginning of modern scholarship, and which it would be impossible to arrest, even if we would. At first, however, to those who have been unacquainted with this scholarship, it seems like dispossession, deprivation.

But not in the end. Let us quote Schweitzer: "Jesus as a concrete historical personality remains a stranger to our time, but his spirit, which lies hidden in his words, is known in simplicity and its influence is direct. . . . He comes to us as One unknown, without a name, as of old, by the lake-side, he came to those men who knew him not. He speaks to us the same word: 'Follow thou me!' and sets us to the tasks which he has to fulfill for our time."[12]

This is the language of mysticism. But also the language of experiential truth. If it is theology, it is theology of the heart, unforced, spontaneous. The theology of which we have complained is the kind that forces history into its pattern. In this passage, it is from facing history *honestly* that we receive a direct impression. If it is mystical, it is also imperatively ethical. The same thing happens as we listen to the Old Testament prophets. It happens with a poem, a moving narrative, a loving deed. It happens frequently in listening to Jesus. In the sense that Schweitzer means here, Jesus does speak to our time.

If Jesus failed in his particular expectation, he did not fail in his total mission. In a larger way than he had thought of, but through trusting implicitly in the God he believed commanded him, he gained an ascendancy over the souls of men that has lasted for many centuries. This is not failure. This is triumph unspeakable. Whatever the difficulties in the way of seeing him clearly as one who moved in history, we know and shall long know that he moves in human life. And he will still be teaching us. We shall still marvel at his faith and courage. We shall still be melted by his love. There is much about him that is lost in the mists. But there is much that can never be lost. He has had the power to attract to himself the adoration of many generations. He will have it still. For there is a spirit that moves through history, and though it be not the spirit of Jesus alone, there is none other through whom it has become so radiantly manifested. We shall still walk with him in Galilee and rejoice that in him the erring and the sinful found a friend. We shall still stand in awe in the Garden of Gethsemane, listening to his prayer: "Thy will be done." And often it will happen that when our minds don't understand, our hearts will.

Conclusion: Is It Gain or Loss for Religion?

It is felt by many, especially some of the clergy, that the new discoveries must be met with hostility and their effect minimized. But there could be a different approach. Must churches always be defensive? Surely, they must sometime recognize that God can work through natural events in a gradual social evolution just as well as in some other way. Indeed, this is the way that he does work. A religion is not one whit the less because it has no supernatural origin, no miracles and not too much uniqueness. What we need is not the victory of one religion over other religions but the recognition of the noble and the good in all religions. It is this and not exclusive claims that will draw the world together and bring mankind towards its needed unity.

Christianity, Judaism, Buddhism, Islam, Taoism—all the high religions, no matter what their claims, have grown in natural ways and evolved with history. It is encouraging that to a large extent, and at their best, they exalt the same principles and plead for the same righteousness and point to love and brotherhood as the path to the good life, both for individuals and for society.

Surely the same God, the same indwelling Spirit, is at work in all. If we would accept more of the living truth and less of the creeds that divide us, perhaps he could work better. If we would break down the barriers that wall us in, perhaps he would have more room to carry on his purpose.

We can have, if we will, a faith that does not seek its basis in unique events: and which does not need the miraculous or supernatural. God is wherever men have found him. He is where men find him still. Wherever truth is spoken, wherever life reveals its wonder and its loveliness, in all goodness, all love and all compassion, and in all brave and generous deeds.

List of Abbreviations Used in References

BA—*Biblical Archeologist*
BASOR—*Bulletin of the American Schools of Oriental Research*
DCG—*Dictionary of Christ and the Gospels*—Hastings
EBi—*Encyclopedia Biblica*
ERE—*Encyclopedia of Religion and Ethics*
HDB—*Dictionary of the Bible*—Hastings
ICC—*International Critical Commentaries*
JQR—*Jewish Quarterly Review*
Peake—*Peake's Commentary on the Bible*
RB—*Revue biblique*

REFERENCES

1. The Discovery of the Scrolls

General:

D. Barthelemy and J. T. Milik, *Discoveries in the Judaean Desert, I, Qumrán Cave I*, Oxford University Press, 1955.

Millar Burrows, *The Dead Sea Scrolls*, Viking Press, 1955.

Mar A. Y. Samuel, "The Purchase of the Jerusalem Scrolls," in BA, Vol. XII, No. 2, May, 1949.

A. Dupont-Sommer, "La Grotte aux manuscrits du Désert de Juda," in *Revue de Paris*, July, 1949, pp. 79–90.

J. C. Trever, "The Discovery of the Scrolls," in BA, 1948, pp. 46–57.

R. de Vaux, "Les Manuscrits hébreux du Désert de Juda," in *La Vie Intellectuelle*, June, 1949, pp. 583–596.

R. de Vaux, "La Cachette des manuscrits hébreux," in RB, lvi, 1949, pp. 234–236.

R. de Vaux, "La Grotte des manuscrits hébreux," *ibid*, lvi, 1949, pp. 586–609.

Edmund Wilson, *The Scrolls from the Dead Sea*, Oxford University Press, 1955.

1. See L.-H. Vincent, in RB, vol. liv, 1947, p. 269.
2. J. C. Trever in *Smithsonian Institution Annual Report*, 1953, pp. 425–435.
3. J. C. Trever, "The Discovery of the Scrolls," *supra;* also BASOR, No. 111, Oct., 1948, pp. 3–16.
4. John Allegro in *Listener* magazine, Feb. 16, 1956.
5. W. L. Reed, "Qumrán Caves Expedition of March, 1952," BASOR, No. 135, Oct., 1954; Millar Burrows, *supra*, Chap. III. For current reports, see *Palestine Exploration Quarterly*, BASOR and BA.
6. A. Dupont-Sommer, *The Jewish Sect of Qumrán and the Essenes*, trans. R. D. Barnett, The Macmillan Company, 1955. See Chap. I and Postscript, pp. 167–170.
7. Flavius Josephus, *Wars of the Jews*, Bk. II, Chap. VIII, 13., T. Nelson & Sons, London, 1873.
8. Millar Burrows, *op. cit.*, pp. 64–69.
9. Edmund Wilson, *supra*, pp. 113–121.
10. New York *Times*, Feb. 10, 1956.
11. New York *Times*, Feb. 25, 1956.

12. The Isaiah Scrolls are described by Millar Burrows, *op. cit.*, p. 19f., and evaluated pp. 301ff.

13. For difficulties and developments in translation of Habakkuk Scroll, see W. H. Brownlee in BASOR, No. 112, Dec., 1948, pp. 8–18; No. 114, April, 1949, pp. 9ff; No. 116, Dec., 1949, pp. 14ff. See also Dupont-Sommer, *op.cit.*, partial translation *passim*. Millar Burrows, *op. cit.*, translation, pp. 365–370.

14. W. H. Brownlee, "The Dead Sea Manual of Discipline," BASOR, Supplementary Studies, Nos. 10–12, 1951. For translation, see Millar Burrows, *op. cit.*, pp. 371–389.

15. For translation, see *ibid.*, pp. 390–399.

16. For translation, see *ibid.*, pp. 400–415.

17. New York *Times*, Feb. 8, 1956.

18. BASOR, Supplementary Studies, No. 10–12, 1951, p. 58.

19. A. Dupont-Sommer, *Dead Sea Scrolls, a Preliminary Survey* (English trans.), Oxford: Basil Blackwell, 1952, p. 100; quoted, Dupont-Sommer, *The Jewish Sect of Qumrân and the Essenes*.

2. The Dating of the Scrolls

General:

W. F. Albright, "On the Date of the Scrolls from Ain Feshka and the Nash Papyrus," BASOR, No. 115, Oct., 1949, pp. 10–19.

S. A. Birnbaum, "The Qumrán Scrolls and Paleography," BASOR, Supplementary Studies Nos. 13–14, 1952.

Millar Burrows, *The Dead Sea Scrolls*, Viking Press, New York, 1955. Chaps. IV, V, and *passim*.

H. H. Rowley, *The Zadokite Fragments and the Dead Sea Scrolls*, The Macmillan Company, 1955; with extensive bibliography.

J. C. Trever, "The Problem of Dating the Dead Sea Scrolls," in *Smithsonian Institution Annual Report*, 1954, pp. 425–435; "A Paleographic Study of the Jerusalem Scrolls," BASOR, No. 113, Feb., 1949, pp. 6–23.

1. S. Zeitlin, "A Commentary on the Book of Habakkuk, Important Discovery or Hoax?" JQR, N.S. xxxix, 1948-1949, pp. 235–247. See also: "Scholarship and the Hoax of Recent Discoveries," *ibid.*, pp. 337–363; "The Alleged Antiquity of the Scrolls," *ibid.*, N.S. xl, 1949-50, pp. 57–78; W. F. Albright, "Are the 'Ain Feshkha Scrolls a Hoax?" *ibid.*, pp. 41–49; Millar Burrows, "A Note on the Recently Discovered MSS," *ibid.*, pp. 51–56. Bibliographies: H. H. Rowley, *supra*; Millar Burrows, *supra*.

2. W. F. Albright, BASOR, No. 115, Oct., 1949, p. 12.

3. See *Vallentine's Jewish Encyclopedia*, London: Shapiro, Vallentine & Co., 1938, p. 345; ERE, vol. VII, 1941, pp. 662ff; Rowley, *op. cit.*

4. See under *General, supra*.

5. See Albright, under *General, supra*.

6. S. A. Birnbaum, "How Old Are the Cave Manuscripts: A Paleographic Discussion," *Vetus Testamentum*, i, 1951, pp. 91–109.

7. See notes in John Trever's article, BASOR, No. 113, Feb., 1949, pp. 6–23.

8. JQR, articles noted in 1, *supra;* other articles in almost every issue of JQR.

9. J. C. Trever, BASOR, No. 113, Feb., 1949, p. 22.

10. Sir Frederick Kenyon, *The Bible and Archaeology*, Harper & Brothers, 1940, pp. 228–229; W. F. Albright on dating of Nash Papyrus, *Journal of Biblical Literature*, vol. lvi, pp. 145–176, Sept., 1937.

11. Millar Burrows, *op. cit.*
12. See O. Braun, *Oriens Christianus*, i, 1901, pp. 299ff.
13. H. H. Rowley, *op. cit.*, Chap. I.
14. *Ibid.*
15. *Ibid.*, p. 2, footnote.
16. See, for example, H. Del Medico, *Deux manuscrits hébreux de la Mer Morte*, Paris: Guenthner, 1951.
17. A. Dupont-Sommer, *The Jewish Sect of Qumrân and the Essenes*, trans. R. D. Barnett, The Macmillan Company, 1955, pp. 5–6.
18 R. de Vaux, "Report to the Académie des Inscriptions et Belles Lettres," April 4, 1952, reported in the *Manchester Guardian*, April 7, 1952.
19. H. H. Rowley, *op. cit.*, p. 18, footnote 5.

3. The Sect of the Scrolls

General:

W. H. Brownlee, "Biblical Interpretation Among the Sectaries of the Dead Sea Scrolls," BA, Vol. XIV, No. 3, Sept., 1951. ICC, ERE, HBD, DCG, EBI, Peake, Abingdon.

R. H. Charles, *Religious Development between the Old and the New Testaments*, Henry Holt, 1913; *The Apocrypha and Pseudepigrapha of the Old Testament, in English*, (2 Vols.) Oxford: The Clarendon Press, 1913.

S. R. Driver, *Introduction to the Literature of the Old Testament*, Charles Scribner's Sons, 1892.

J. G. Frazer, *Folk-lore in the Old Testament*, London: The Macmillan Company, Ltd.; 1919.

P. Haupt, ed., *The Sacred Books of the Old Testament in Hebrew. A New English Translation*. New York, 1898 ff.

H. F. Hamilton, *The People of God*, Vol. I, *Israel*.

G. A. Smith, *The Historical Geography of the Holy Land*, A. C. Armstrong and Son, 1896.

W. R. Smith, *The Religion of the Semites*, The Macmillan Company, 1927; *The Prophets of Israel*, Edinburgh: A. and C. Black, 1882.

Westminster Historical Atlas to the Bible, Westminster Press, 1945.

1. S. R. Driver, *supra;* Peake, "Introduction to the Pentateuch."
2. Peake, pp. 135ff; numerous articles, ERE; ICC, "Genesis"; Andree, *Die Flutsagen, ethnographisch betrachet*, Brunswick, 1891, much used in HDB, II, 16–23.
3. Articles, ERE, EBI; Peake, p. 51.
4. *Westminster Atlas, supra.*
5. Peake, p. 62a.
6. *Journal of Victoria Institute*. Vol. XXVIII, p. 267; *ibid.* Vol. XXVI, p. 12; HDB, p. 802b.
7. Peake, p. 64b.
8. A. H. M'Neile in Peake, p. 64b.
9. *Ibid.*
10. See W. R. Smith, *supra;* A. B. Davidson, *Old Testament Prophecy*, Edinburgh: T. and T. Clark, 1904; W. G. Jordan, *Prophetic Ideas and Ideals*. Numerous articles in encyclopedias and commentaries.
11. For method and results of the modern scientific textual and historical criticism, see S. R. Driver, *op. cit.* and articles in Peake.
12. For dating of Deuteronomy, see T. W. Davies in Peake, pp. 231ff, also ICC.
13. Articles: "Priests," HDB; "Chief Priests," "High Priest," DCG.
14. Articles: HDB; EBI; all encyclopedias.
15. J. P. Smyth, *How We Got Our Bible*, Harper & Brothers, 1899, **1912**;

The Old Documents and the New Bible, J. Pott & Co., 1890. Articles in encyclopedias under "Text of the New Testament," etc. HDB, IV, pp. 732–740.

16. R. H. Charles, *The Apocrypha and Pseudepigrapha of the Old Testament, in English, supra.* Leading scholar in this field; has articles in EBI, DCG; see also his *Eschatology*, London: A. C. Black, 1899.

17. A. W. Streane, *The Age of the Maccabees*, London: Eyre & Spottiswood, 1898; E. Schürer, *The Jewish People in the Time of Jesus Christ*, Edinburgh; T. & T. Clark, 1897–98. Articles: EBI, HDB, ERE, etc., on all aspects of Hellenism in relation to Judaism.

18. Flavius Josephus, *Antiquities of the Jews*, XVIII, i, 6. T. Nelson & Sons, London, 1873. (See Appendix).

19. For this entire section, see H. H. Rowley, *The Zadokite Fragments and the Dead Sea Scrolls*, The Macmillan Company, 1953; A Dupont-Sommer, *The Jewish Sect of Qumrân and the Essenes*, trans. R. D. Barnett, The Macmillan Company, 1955; Millar Burrows, *The Dead Sea Scrolls*, Viking Press, 1955; numerous articles cited in bibliographies of the above.

20. Discussed in works named in 19, *supra.* Also extensively in BASOR, BA, etc. See W. H. Brownlee, *supra;* and BA, Vol. XIV, No. 3, Sept., 1951.

21. Millar Burrows, *op. cit.*, p. 185f.

22. A Dupont-Sommer, *op. cit.*, pp. 54–57.

23. *Ibid.*

24. Millar Burrows, *op. cit.*, pp. 259–260.

25. A. S. Peake, *Problem of Suffering in the Old Testament*, Alec Allenson, 1947; Giesebrecht, *Beitrage zur Jesaiakritik*, pp. 146–185, Commentaries.

26. W. H. Brownlee, "The Servant of the Lord in the Qumrân Scrolls," BASOR, Nos. 132 and 135, Dec., 1953 and Oct., 1954; for passage cited, see No. 135, pp. 34–35.

27. G. A. Smith, *supra*, p. 504.

28. *Ibid*, p. 499.

29. Flavius Josephus, *Wars of the Jews*, II, VIII, 10. London: T. Nelson & Sons, 1873.

4. The Scrolls and Christian Origins

General:

S. Angus, *The Mystery-Religions and Christianity*, Charles Scribner's Sons, 1925.

W. H. Brownlee, *The Dead Sea Manual of Discipline*, translated and annotated; BASOR, Supplementary Studies, Nos. 10–12, 1951.

Millar Burrows, translations of Scrolls in *The Dead Sea Scrolls*, Viking Press, 1955.

E. Carpenter, *Pagan and Christian Creeds*, Harcourt, Brace and Company, 1921.

C. Clemen, *Primitive Christianity and Its Non-Jewish Sources*, Edinburgh: T. and T. Clark, 1912.

A. Dupont-Sommer, *The Jewish Sect of Qumrân and the Essenes*, trans. R. D. Barnett, The Macmillan Company, 1955. Translations *passim.*

Hawkins, *Horae Synopticae.*

M. R. James, *The Apocryphal New Testament*, Oxford University Press, 1924. Translated and annotated.

J. Moffatt, *An Introduction to the Literature of the New Testament*, Charles Scribner's Sons, 1925.

G. Murray, *Five Stages of Greek Religion*, Columbia University Press, 1925; The Beacon Press, 1952.

B. F. Westcott and F. J. A. Hort, *The New Testament in the Original Greek*. Macmillan & Company, 1885.

1. Millar Burrows, *supra*, p. 343.
2. See J. Moffatt, *supra*, or articles in EBI, DCG; Peake, etc.
3. HDB, extra vol., p. 471ff.
4. M. R. James, *supra*, pp. 90, 92–93.
5. See HDB, Vol. III, p. 203ff; F. C. Conybeare, *Myth, Magic and Morals*, Chap. XII, London: Watts & Co., 1909.
6. See ICC; Century Bible; Peake, "Matthew."
7. G. Murray, *supra;* E. Carpenter, *supra*. Articles in Peake.
8. J. G. Frazer, *The Golden Bough* (3rd ed.) London: Macmillan and Company, Ltd., 1951. *Folk-lore in the Old Testament*, London: Macmillan and Company, Ltd., 1919; G. Murray, *op. cit.*
9. D. Howlett, "Faith and History" in the *Atlantic Monthly*, April, 1956.
10. F. M. Cross, Jr., "The Scrolls and the New Testament," in the *Christian Century*, August 24, 1956.
11. *Ibid.*
12. A. Dupont-Sommer, *supra*, p. 39.
13. *Christian Century*, note 10 *supra*, p. 971.
14. HDB, Vol. IV, p. 722ff.
15. A. Dupont-Sommer, *op. cit.*, p. 39.
16. Quoted by A. Dupont-Sommer, *ibid*, p. 165. See R. H. Charles's article on the *Testaments* in HDB.
17. R. H. Charles, *The Apocrypha and Pseudepigrapha of the Old Testament in English*, II, pp. 282, 291–292, Oxford: The Clarendon Press, 1913.
18. *Ibid*, p. 166.
19. The *Didaché* is treated in HDB, extra volume. Also R. H. Charles, *op. cit.;* ERE.
20. Text and translation in J. B. Lightfoot's *Apostolic Fathers*, Macmillan and Company, 1889. See also *Dictionary of Christian Biograph and Literature*, Little, Brown & Company, 1911.
21. See the Commentaries. Church-connected scholars often dislike to abandon the possibility that John and the Synoptics may somehow be reconciled, but the reader can judge for himself how insuperable are the difficulties. For brief factual presentation of the problem, see particularly Peake, p. 743.
22. Millar Burrows, *op. cit.*, p. 388.
23. *Zeitschrift fur Theologie and Kirche*, XLVII (1950) Heft. 2, p. 209.
24. Eusebius Pamphili, *Historica Ecclesiastica*, II, 23. See M. J. Routh, *Reliquiae Sacrae*, Oxford, 1814–1818.
25. *Ibid*, II, 1.
26. EBI, HDB, "Nazareth," "Nazarene," "Nazarite" (DCG inadequate).
27. G. Murray, *op. cit.*, Columbia University Press edition, p. 196.

5. The Scrolls and Jesus

General:

A. Edersheim, *Life and Times of Jesus, the Messiah*, Longmans, Green & Co., 1907.
R. Graves and J. Podro, *The Nazarene Gospel Restored*, Doubleday & Co., 1954.
J. Klausner, *Jesus of Nazareth*, The Macmillan Company, 1926.
E. Renan, *Life of Jesus*, The Modern Library, 1927.
W. Sanday, *The Life of Christ in Recent Research*, Oxford: The Clarendon Press, 1899.

A. Schweitzer, *The Quest of the Historical Jesu;*, The Macmillan Company, 1948.

W. B. Smith, *Der vorchristliche Jesus: Ecce Deus.* (Against the canonical viewpoint.)

B. H. Streeter, *The Four Gospels*, The Macmillan Company, 1925.

J. Weiss, *Jesus von Nazareth, Mythos oder Geschichte.* (In defense of the canonical viewpoint.)

1. All lives of Jesus are largely out of date owing to the new discoveries. Renan's, however, is still rewarding reading. Edersheim is an excellent standard work. Graves and Podro's book is an attempt to restore "the original gospel": a massive work of brilliant scholarship. No "popular" lives of Jesus are worth anything to the researcher and not many are worth anything to anyone else.

2. A. Schweitzer, *supra.*

3. See articles: "Eschatology," "Messiah," etc., in EBI, HDB, DCG, etc., and ICC and Cambridge commentaries on Matthew.

4. See, e. g., A. Schweitzer, *op. cit.*, on Renan, *passim.*

5. A good example of the liberal (trinitarian) lives of Jesus is T. R. Glover's *The Jesus of History*, Association Press, 1917. More adventurous is J. Middleton Murry's *Jesus, Man of Genius.* New York and London: Harper & Brothers, 1926.

6. A. Schweitzer, *op. cit.*, p. 370.

7. This passage in Isaiah, if not familiar, should be read; discussion of it has been very wide. See Commentaries.

8. See articles on "John the Baptist" in EBI, HDB, etc.

9. Mark xv, 34. Many attempts have been made to explain away this cry of despair, beginning with Gospel writers: see Mark xv, 35–36.

10. DCG, I, 504b.

11. See J. Moffatt's translation of the New Testament for a good approximation of *koiné* Greek.

12. A. Schweitzer, *op. cit.*, pp. 401, 403.

APPENDIX

Ancient Descriptions of the Essenes

1. By Philo of Alexandria, in *Quod Omnis Probus Liber,* written circa 20 A.D.

They were a sect of Jews, and lived in Syria Palestine, over 4000 in number, and called Essæi, because of their saintliness; for *hosio*=saintly, is the same word as Essæus. Worshippers of God, they yet did not sacrifice animals, regarding a reverent mind as the only true sacrifice. At first they lived in villages and avoided cities, in order to escape the contagion of evils rife therein. They pursued agriculture and other peaceful arts; but accumulated not gold or silver, nor owned mines. No maker of warlike weapons, no huckster or trader by land or sea, was to be found among them. Least of all were any slaves found among them; for they saw in slavery a violation of the law of nature, which made all men free brethren, one of the other.

Abstract philosophy and logic they eschewed, except so far as it could subserve ethical truth and practice. Natural philosophy they only studied so far as it teaches that there is a God who made and watches over all things. Moral philosophy or ethic was their chief preoccupation, and their conduct was regulated by their national (Jewish) laws. These laws they especially studied on the seventh day, which they held holy, leaving off all work upon it and meeting in their synagogues, as these places of resort were called. In them they sat down in ranks, the older ones above the younger. Then one took and read the Bible, while the rest listened attentively; and another, who was very learned in the Bible, would expound whatever was obscure in the lesson read, explaining most things in their time-honoured fashion by means of symbols. They were taught piety, holiness, justice, the art of regulating home and city, knowledge of what is really good and bad and of what is indifferent, what ends to avoid, what to pursue,—in short, love of God, of virtue, and of man.

And such teaching bore fruit. Their life-long purity, their avoiding of oaths or falsehood, their recognition of a good providence alone, showed their love of God. Their love of virtue revealed itself in their indifference to money, worldly position, and pleasure. Their love of man in their kindliness, their equality, their fellowship passing all words. For no one had his private house, but shared his dwelling with all; and, living as they did in colonies (the tasous), they threw open their doors to any of their sect who came their way. They had a storehouse, common expenditure, common raiments, common food eaten in Syssitia or common meals. This was made possible by their practice of putting whatever they each earned day by day into a common fund, out of which also the sick were supported when they could not work. The aged among them were objects of reverence and honour, and treated by the rest as parents by real children.

Eusebius (circa 300 A.D.) quotes Philo as saying that the Essenes inhabited many cities of Judea, as well as many villages and populated tracts. Their tenets, he continues, are espoused by them of free choice and not as a matter of race.

In probable reference to the Essenes:

Even in our own day, there are still men whose only guide is God; men who live by the true reason of nature, not only themselves free, but filling their neighbours with a spirit of freedom. They are not very numerous indeed. But that is not strange. For the highest nobility is ever rare; and then these men have turned aside from the vulgar herd to devote themselves to a contemplation of nature's verities. They pray, if it were possible, that they may reform our fallen lives; but, if they cannot, owing to the tide of evils and wrongs which surges up in cities, they flee away, lest they too be swept off their feet by the force of its current. And we, if we had a true zeal for self-improvement, would have to track them to their places of retreat, and, halting as suppliants before them, would beseech them to come to us and tame our life, grown too fierce and wild; preaching, instead of war and slavery and untold ills, their gospel of peace and freedom, and all the fulness of other blessings.

2. By Pliny the Elder (circa 70 A.D.), in *Historica Naturalis*, book v, chapter 17.

The Hessenes live on the W. side away from the shores (of the Dead Sea), out of reach of their baneful influences. A solitary race, and strange above all others in the entire world. They live without women, renouncing all sexual love. They eschew money, and live among the palm-trees. Yet the number of their fellows (convenarum) is kept up and day by day renewed; for there flock to them from afar many who, wearied of battling with the rough sea of life, drift into their system. Thus for thousands of ages (strange to tell) the race is perpetuated, and yet no one is born in it. So does the contrition felt by others for their past life enrich this set of men. Below them lay Engadi, a town once second only to Jerusalem in its fertility and groves of palms. Now 'tis but one more tomb. Next comes Masada, a fort on a rock, and, like the former, not far from the Dead Sea. And here ends our account of Judea.

3. By Josephus

For there are three philosophical sects among the Jews. The followers of the first of whom are the Pharisees; of the second the Sadducees; and the third sect, who pretends to a severer discipline, are called Essens. These last are Jews by birth, and seem to have a greater affection for one another than the other sects have. These Essens reject pleasures as an evil, but esteem continence, and the conquest over our passions, to be virtue. They neglect wedlock, but choose out other persons' children, while they are pliable, and fit for learning; and esteem them to be of their kindred, and form them according to their own manners. They do not absolutely deny the fitness of marriage, and the succession of mankind thereby continued; but they guard against the lascivious behaviour of women, and are persuaded that none of them preserve their fidelity to one man.

These men are despisers of riches, and so very communicative as raises our admiration. Nor is there any one to be found among them who hath more than another; for it is a law among them, that those who come to them must let what they have be common to the whole order,—insomuch, that among them all there is no appearance of poverty or excess of riches, but every one's possessions are intermingled with every other's possessions; and so there is, as it were, one patrimony among all the brethren. They think that oil is a defilement; and if any one of them be anointed without his own approbation, it is wiped off his body; for they think to be sweaty is a good thing, as they do also to be clothed in white garments. They also have stewards appointed to take care of their common affairs, who every one of them have no separate business for any, but what is for the use of them all.

They have no certain city, but many of them dwell in every city; and if any of their sect come from other places, what they have lies open for them, just as if it were their own; and they go into such as they never knew before, as if they had been ever so long acquainted with them. For which reason they carry nothing with them when they travel into remote parts, though still they take their weapons with them, for fear of thieves. Accordingly there is, in every city where they live, one appointed particularly to take care of strangers, and to provide garments and other necessaries for them. But the habit and management of their bodies is such as children use who are in fear of their masters. Nor do they allow of the change of garments, or of shoes, till they be first entirely torn to pieces, or worn out by time. Nor do they either buy or sell any thing to one another; but every one of them gives what he hath to him that wanteth it; and receives from him again in lieu of it what may be convenient for himself; and although there be no requital made, they are fully allowed to take what they want of whomsoever they please.

And as for their piety towards God, it is very extraordinary; for before sun-rising they speak not a word about profane matters, but put up certain prayers which they have received from their forefathers, as if they made a supplication for its rising. After this, every one of them are sent away by their curators, to exercise some of those arts wherein they are skilled, in which they labour with great diligence till the fifth hour. After which they assemble themselves together again into one place; and when they have clothed themselves in white veils, they then bathe their bodies in cold water. And after this purification is over, they every one meet together in an apartment of their own, into which it is not permitted to any of another sect to enter; while they go, after a pure manner, into the dining-room, as into a certain holy temple, and quietly set themselves down; upon which the baker lays them loaves in order; the cook also brings a single plate of one sort of food, and sets it before every one of them; but a priest says grace before meat; and it is unlawful for any one to taste of the food before grace be said. The same priest, when he hath dined, says grace again after meat; and when they begin, and when they end, they praise God, as he that bestows their food upon them; after which they lay aside their [white] garments, and betake themselves to their labours again till the evening; then they return home to supper, after the same manner; and if there be any strangers there, they sit down with them. Nor is there ever any clamour or disturbance to pollute their house, but they give every one leave to speak in his turn; which silence thus kept in their house, appears to foreigners like some tremendous mystery; the cause of which is that perpetual sobriety they exercise, and the same settled measure of meat and drink that is allotted to them, and that such as is abundantly sufficient for them.

And truly, as for other things, they do nothing but according to the injunctions of their curators; only these two things are done among them at every one's own free will, which are, to assist those that want it, and to shew mercy; for they are permitted of their own accord to afford succour to such as deserve it, when they stand in need of it, and to bestow food on those that are in distress, but they cannot give any thing to their kindred without the curators. They dispense their anger after a just manner, and restrain their passion. They are eminent for fidelity, and are the ministers of peace; whatsoever they say also is firmer than an oath; but swearing is avoided by them, and they esteem it worse than perjury; for they say, that he who cannot be believed without [swearing by] God, is already condemned. They also take great pains in studying the writings of the ancients, and choose out of them what is most for the advantage of their soul and body; and they inquire after such roots and medicinal stones as may cure their distempers.

But now, if any one hath in mind to come over to their sect, he is not immediately admitted, but he is prescribed the same method of living which they use, for a year, while he continues excluded; and they give him a small hatchet, and the forementioned girdle, and the white garment. And when he hath given evidence, during that time, that he can observe their continence, he approaches nearer to their way of living, and is made a partaker of the waters of purification; yet is he not even now admitted to live with them; for after this demonstration of his fortitude, his temper is tried two more years, and if he appear to be worthy, they then admit him into their society. And before he is allowed to touch their common food, he is obliged to take tremendous oaths; that, in the first place, he will exercise piety towards God; and then, that he will observe justice towards men; and that he will do no harm to any one, either of his own accord, or by the command of others; that he will always hate the wicked, and be assistant to the righteous; that he will ever show fidelity to all men, and especially to those in authority, because no one obtains the government without God's assistance; and that if he be in authority, he will at no time whatever abuse his authority, nor endeavour to outshine his subjects, either in his garments, or any other finery; that he will be perpetually a lover of truth, and propose to himself to reprove those that tell lies; that he will keep his hands clear from theft, and his soul from unlawful gains; and that he will neither conceal any thing from those of his own sect, nor discover any of their doctrines to others, no, not though any one should compel him so to do at the hazard of his life. Moreover, he swears to communicate their doctrines to no one any otherwise than as he received them himself; that he will abstain from robbery, and will equally preserve the books belonging to their sect, and the names of the angels [or messengers]. These are the oaths by which they secure their proselytes to themselves.

But for those that are caught in any heinous sins, they cast them out of their society; and he who is thus separated from them, does often die after a miserable manner; for as he is bound by the oath he hath taken, and by the customs he hath been engaged in, he is not at liberty to partake of that food that he meets with elsewhere, but is forced to eat grass, and to famish his body with hunger till he perish; for which reason they receive many of them again when they are at their last gasp, out of compassion to them, as thinking the miseries they have endured till they came to the very brink of death, to be a sufficient punishment for the sins they had been guilty of.

But in the judgments they exercise they are most accurate and just; nor do they pass sentence by the votes of a court that is fewer than a hundred. And as to what is once determined by that number, it is unalterable. What they most of all honour, after God himself, is the name of their legislator [Moses]; whom, if any one blaspheme, he is punished capitally. They also think it a good thing to obey their elders, and the major part. According-ly, if ten of them be sitting together, no one of them will speak while the other nine are against it. They also avoid spitting in the midst of them, or on the right side. Moreover, they are stricter than any other of the Jews in resting from their labours on the seventh day; for they not only get their food ready the day be-fore, that they may not be obliged to kindle a fire on that day, but they will not remove any vessel out of its place, nor go to stool thereon. Nay, on the other days, they dig a small pit, a foot deep, with a paddle (which kind of hatchet is given them when they are first admitted among them); and covering themselves round with their garment, that they may not affront the divine rays of light, they ease themselves into that pit, after which they put the earth that was dug out again into the pit; and even this they do only in the more lonely places, which they choose out for this purpose; and although this easement of the body be natural, yet it is a rule with them to wash themselves after it, as if it were a defilement to them.

Now after the time of their preparatory trial is over, they are parted into four classes; and so far are the juniors inferior to the seniors, that if the seniors should be touched by the juniors, they must wash themselves, as if they had intermixed themselves with the company of a foreigner. They are long-lived also; insomuch that many of them live above a hundred years, by means of the simplicity of their diet; nay, as I think, by means of the regular course of life they observe also. They contemn the miseries of life, and are above pain, by the generosity of their mind. And as for death, if it will be for their glory, they esteem it better than living always; and indeed our war with the Romans gave abun-dant evidence what great souls they had in their trials, wherein, although they were tortured and distorted, burnt and torn to pieces, and went through all kinds of instruments of torment, that they might be forced either to blaspheme their legislator, or to eat what was forbidden them, yet could they not be made to do either of them, no, nor once to flatter their tormentors, or to shed a tear; but they smiled in their very pains, and laughed those to scorn who inflicted the torments upon them, and resigned up their souls with great alacrity, as expecting to receive them again.

For their doctrine is this:—That bodies are corruptible, and that the matter they are made of is not permanent; but that the souls are immortal, and continue for ever; and that they come out of the most subtile air, and are united to their bodies as in prisons, into which they are drawn by a certain natural enticement; but that when they are set free from the bonds of the flesh, they then, as released from a long bondage, rejoice and mount upward. And this is like the opinion of the Greeks, that good souls have their habitations beyond the ocean, in a region that is neither oppressed with storms of rain, or snow, or with intense heat, but that this place is such as is refreshed by the gentle breathing of a west wind, that is perpetually blowing from the ocean; while they allot to bad souls a dark and tempestuous den, full of never-ceasing punishments. And indeed the Greeks seem to me to have followed the same notion, when they allot the islands of the blessed to their brave men, whom they call heroes and demi-gods; and to the souls of the wicked, the region of the ungodly, in Hades, where their fables relate that certain persons, such as Sisyphus, and Tantalus, and Ixion, and Tityus, are punished; which is built on this first supposition, that souls are immortal; and thence are those exhortations to virtue, and dehortations from wickedness collected; whereby good men are bettered in the conduct of their life, by the hope they have of reward after their death, and whereby the vehement inclinations of bad men to vice are restrained, by the fear and expectation they are in, that although they should lie concealed in this life, they should suffer immortal punishment after their death. These are the divine doctrines of the Essens about the soul, which lay an unavoidable bait for such as have once had a taste of their philosophy.

There are also those among them who undertake to foretell things to come, by reading the holy books, and using several sorts of purifications, and being perpetually conversant in the discourses of the prophets; and it is but seldom that they miss in their predictions.

Moreover, there is another order of Essens, who agree with the rest as to their way of living, and customs, and laws, but differ from them in the point of marriage, as thinking that by not marrying they cut off the principal part of human life, which is the prospect of succession; nay rather, that if all men should be of the same opinion, the whole race of mankind would fail. However, they try their spouses for three years; and if they find that they have their natural purgations thrice, as trials that they are likely to be fruitful, they then actually marry them. But they do not use to accompany with their wives when they are with child, as a demonstration that they do not marry out of regard to pleasure, but for the sake of posterity. Now the women go into the baths with some of their garments on, as the men do with somewhat girded about them. And these are the customs of this order of Essens.

—Wars of the Jews, Book II, viii, 2-14

At this time there were three sects among the Jews, who had different opinions concerning human actions; the one was called the sect of the Pharisees, another the sect of the Sadducees, and the other the sect of the Essens. Now for the Pharisees, they say that some actions, but not all, are the work of fate, and some of them are in our own power, and that they are liable to fate, but are not caused by fate. But the sect of the Essens affirm, that fate governs all things, and that nothing befals men but what is according to its determination. And for the Sadducees, they take away fate, and say there is no such thing, and that the events of human affairs are not at its disposal; but they suppose that all our actions are in our own power, so that we are ourselves the causes of what is good, and receive what is evil from our own folly. However, I have given a more exact account of these opinions in the second book of the Jewish War.

—Antiquities of the Jews, Book XIII, v, 9

The doctrine of the Essens is this: That all things are best ascribed to God. They teach the immortality of souls, and esteem that the rewards of righteousness are to be earnestly striven for; and when they send what they have dedicated to God into the temple, they do not offer sacrifices, because they have more pure lustrations of their own; on which account they are excluded from the common court of the temple, but offer their sacrifices themselves; yet is their course of life better than that of other men; and they entirely addict themselves to husbandry. It also deserves our admiration, how much they exceed all other men that addict themselves to virtue, and this in righteousness: and indeed to such a degree, that as it hath never appeared among any other men, neither Greeks nor barbarians, no, not for a little time, so hath it endured a long while among them. This is demonstrated by that institution of theirs, which will not suffer any thing to hinder them from having all things in common; so that a rich man enjoys no more of his own wealth than he who hath nothing at all. There are about four thousand men that live in this way, and neither marry wives, nor are desirous to keep servants; as thinking the latter tempts men to be unjust, and the former gives the handle to domestic quarrels; but as they live by themselves, they minister to one another. They also appoint certain stewards to receive the incomes of their revenues, and of the fruits of the ground; such as are good men and priests, who are to get their corn and their food ready for them. They none of them differ from others of the Essens in their way of living, but do the most resemble those Dacæ who are called *Polistæ* [dwellers in cities].

—Antiquities of the Jews, Book XVIII, i, 5

Now there was one of these Essens, whose name was Manahem, who had this testimony, that he not only conducted his life after an excellent manner, but had the foreknowledge of future events given him by God also. This man once saw Herod when he was a child, and going to school, and saluted him as king of the Jews; . . . Now at that time Herod did not at all attend to what Manahem said, as having no hopes of such advancement; but a little afterward, when he was so fortunate as to be advanced to the dignity of king, and was in the height of his dominion, he sent for Manahem, and asked him how long he should reign. Manahem did not tell him the full length of his reign; wherefore, upon that silence of his, he asked him farther, whether he should reign ten years or not? He replied, "Yes, twenty, nay, thirty years"; but did not assign the just determinate limit of his reign. Herod was satisfied with these replies, and gave Manahem his hand, and dismissed him; and from that time he continued to honour all the Essens. We have thought it proper to relate these facts to our readers, how strange soever they be, and to declare what hath happened among us, because many of these Essens have, by their excellent virtue, been thought worthy of this knowledge of divine revelations.

—Antiquities of the Jews, Book XV, x, 5